Doing Good
While Doing Well™

How real estate investors provide a service and make a difference

By

Lou Brown

&

**Local Certified Affordable Housing
Providers**

Table of Contents

Introduction

Welcome to the first day of the rest of your life! I say that knowing that many of you reading this are embarking on a new journey. Real estate is brand-new and foreign to you. And you are getting involved for one important reason – financial freedom for yourself and your family.

Perhaps you are like so many others that have seen what the corporate world can do and realized an important axiom (and one that I have lived my life by) – "If it is to be it is up to me!"

What's surprising to many people is that making money in real estate is like any other business- It's based on a formula.

Those who have failed in real estate have failed because they did not follow a known proven business model – which is nothing more than a formula. They followed their own plan. And as far as I'm concerned, running a business without a model is like building a house without blueprints.

If you look at my track record in the real estate industry, you will see that I am known as an innovator. If something is not working in the real estate industry, I like to look at it from all angles, tear it apart, see what does and does not work, then put it back together again – only this time in a way that will actually work.

I applaud those of you who have made the decision to move forward in real estate investing, even though some of you reading this are still filled with a little bit of fear and apprehension. That's ok. It's normal. Do you think my first business deal went smoothly? No, baby! Going out on your own, into any unknown business has the slightest possibility that you could fail and lose everything you worked so hard for. But it's not a reason to give up before you even try. My colleagues and I will be showing and proving that this fear can be overcome by proven solutions that already exist.

For example, what if I could show and tell you that with X amount of investment you can get X amount of leads that will yield X amount of deals that will yield XX amount of profit? That's a pretty profound statement, yet it is true. In fact, it's somewhat magical.

But before that can happen, obtaining the right education and tools is critical. Think about college - they don't just deliver a diploma after you've paid the big fat check. First you have to get the recommended textbooks and go through a number of classes. Then and only then can you move to the business world and seek a job in your chosen profession. The sad thing is, even with all the studying and diploma, most people do not end up with a long-term job in their chosen arena.

In business there is a short circuit to the whole process. It's called a franchise. Someone else has already been there, done that, proven the straight path to the money, and has developed a plan that allows others to follow that path - and boy does that make all the difference!

It's pretty profound and one that works for a lot of people - but the franchisee must apply the tools and education they have been given in order to be successful.

Over time, that is what has been developed in real estate. The Certified Affordable Housing Provider® program is designed to short-circuit the process of learning the who, what, where, when and how of making money in real estate.

Join me now as you meet other people who are just like you – they wanted a better life than the one they had!

Simply put - they wanted a better life. They liked the concept of 'Doing Good While Doing Well ^{tm}' and committed to follow the formula to attain sustainable success.

At the end of this book I'm going to invite you to do the same! See you at the top!

Best, Lou

"Take up one idea. Make that one idea your life - think of it, dream of it, and live on that idea. Let the brain, muscles, nerves, every part of your body, be full of that idea, and just leave every other idea alone. This is the way to success."

~ Swami Vivekananda~

Chapter 1

Doing Good While Doing Well
By Lou Brown

"If it is to be - it is up to me!"

Our business inspires me!

That's a rare statement for a lot of business owners to make. But for me, it is absolutely true. I think back to when I was a kid. There are two distinct things I remember from my childhood. Money was tough, and I really had no one to fall back on.

My mom had made some bad decisions about life partners, and it ended up being just her and me against the world. Now this was back in the day when there were not a lot of government programs to help out. I'm not sure, but I don't think it would've mattered. My mother was proud, and did not really want or seek help from others.

You see, my mom was from Scotland. She came over as a war bride, and all of her family was in Scotland. We were estranged from my father, and hence, his entire family. So that just left us.

I know what it's like to have no money. I know what it's like to hide out from the rent man. My mom would say "shhh, don't say anything... I'll have the money by this weekend." She just didn't want to face anyone and have to say that.

Now I didn't know it then, but the universe was starting it's alignment with my journey in life.

Doing Good While Doing Well

I never will forget the one time we went to see some of her friends. I called them aunts and uncles, as I had none. I was about eight years old and Aunt Mabel told me a story. She said they had just bought the duplex they lived in. She told me they went to the bank, got a loan, and that the people on the other side were paying enough money in rent the cover the mortgage. What did she just say?? Even at that age I realized what she said was that they were living there for free!!

Can you imagine how that captured my imagination? Now of course, I didn't know anything about finances or money or how other people even lived. The one thing I did know was - *we* didn't have the money for rent sometimes, and *she* didn't have to pay any.

That's probably where I got the first insight that there really are parallel universes out there. Some people struggle with money and others don't. Some people put forth the effort to think and educate themselves and uncover truths that are unknown to those who do not.

Wow! So all I have to do is remember that there are people fortunate enough to apply themselves and in return, get pieces of information that allow them to break the money code.

The Money Code

The money code is quite fascinating. I am definitely a student of it. Some people work their entire lives and end up with very little to show for it, while others seem to effortlessly move through life and always have plenty of money to spend. So, what's the difference?

Doing Good While Doing Well

I recall that my mother (God rest her soul) was one of the ones who did not take the time or gain the tools to master money - Money mastered her. I did not like the process, and saw how high interest on borrowed money could eat a fortune in a hurry.

So I watched and studied the processes involved. We visited Aunt Mabel and she told us she had bought the duplex next door and that the people on that side were paying enough in rent to cover the mortgage, with enough left over to go into their pockets. I watched their lifestyle change: a new Cadillac every other year, nice furniture, trips and cruises. And they ate out at the steakhouse almost every night!

They just kept buying real estate. One day Aunt Mabel called me and asked me to help her move. They had just bought a brand-new house. It was a two-story, all brick home, in a brand-new subdivision, on a corner lot. Far more house than she, Uncle George, and their two Chihuahuas needed.

"How did you do this, Mabel?" was my question. She said two words that changed my life: **Accumulate Property.**

Now, this parallel universe continued. When I was about 12 years old, my mother heard about a program that would allow us to buy a home. It was a modest three-bedroom home. It was very exciting and things looked positive. Then after form after form were completed and time passed, we were told that she did not qualify.

This devastated her. She didn't say much, but I could tell it really took the wind out of her sails. It was something that she wanted for me. She wanted me out of those apartments – those terrible apartments – and get me into something better, more room, a better location and in turn, a better life.

That was not to be. It affected her so badly that she never tried again.

Several years later when I was about 18 years, old Aunt Mabel said to me "hey, you need to buy a house." I said "yeah, that would be nice, Aunt Mabel, but you've bought all your property by qualifying for loans. I can't qualify my way out of a paper bag."

She laughed and said I needed to meet her friend 'Realtor Sue.' One phone call and realtor Sue was anxious to show me some property. You see, I had worked very hard during my teenage years. I had first started a paper route when I was 11 years old (actually, I was not supposed to start till 12, but I fibbed a bit.) I wanted to get ahead, and I figured this was a chance.

Every chance I got I saved up money and worked after school jobs and did other things to make things work. I knew one thing – I wanted a better life for myself and my mom.

It didn't take long until realtor Sue found a house that I liked. Turns out, I could buy this house differently than Aunt Mabel did.

Again I discovered a parallel universe: those who go to banks and qualify for loans and buy property, versus those who buy property a different way.

And the second way made all the difference.

Essentially…. it's to use the seller as the bank.

I ended up buying my first property at the age of 19, without even going to a bank or qualifying for a loan. That was a real eye-opener!

My mother became my first tenant, paying me $100 per month (along with washing some clothes and cooking some meals. ☺) It was a good deal for me because it helped make ends meet, but it was also a good deal for her. Our rent was about $600 per month, and I told her to take $500 per month and put it towards her debt. Within a year and a half she was debt-free for the rest of her life. That was a new experience for her.

I got to see first-hand that if my mother had discovered this other universe when I was 12 years old, then I would not have spent my teenage years in an apartment.

Knowledge is power. In fact, I teach that 'Knowledge is Power *and Money*.'

As time passed, I was transferred by the company I worked for from Charlotte, North Carolina to Atlanta, Georgia. Why not? My mom was all set and the company offered to pay my closing costs if I would sell my house and buy a new one down there. So I did, and in the process I was surprised to see that in less than two years my property had gone up by 37%!

In Atlanta I again decided not to qualify for a loan, even though I could have. I told the agent to find me a house where the seller would be the bank.

Once again it happened, and to this day I have **never** qualified for a loan from a bank for a single-family or small multifamily property. There was - and is - no reason to. Why would I?

I also started to realize that if I offered my real estate the same way to the people who wanted to live there, then I could help change their lives as well. Why should they be relegated to being renters for the rest of their lives?

I could become the bank for them as the seller, and give them what I would eventually call "The Path to Home Ownership.'®

Inspiration

I started this story with "Our Business Inspires Me!" Likely now you can understand why I think so. Imagine working with a couple or a family and showing them that there is another way.

Imagine giving them a leg up in life and an opportunity that no one else has given them. Imagine working with them to help them improve their credit to the point that they can get a new loan. Or just be the bank for them and give them pride of ownership and the opportunity of possibility.

I have so many stories of people we have helped. One was a 63 years old gentleman who had never owned a home in his name in his life. He started out with our *Work for Equity Program* and did all the repairs to the home with the help of his family and friends. We credited that work towards his down payment. This allowed him the opportunity to work with a credit repair program and get his credit cleaned up so that he could get a new bank loan.

Another success story was a nurse. She loved the idea of our *Work for Equity Program* and even though she didn't have a lot of experience, she went to training sessions at the local builder supply store and learned how to do her own tile and sheet rock work. She transformed her home and made it look absolutely beautiful. We became the bank for her, and have been her bank for over five years now.

Doing Good While Doing Well

We also have a couple in the Chattanooga, Tennessee area that lived in a mobile home on her father's land for over 20 years. We had a beautiful home available on 5 acres of land, and have become the bank for these nice people for the past four years.

The stories are endless, and the challenges that human beings face are much more intense than I had to face.

People who are selling their homes are drawn to our program. They see that the home that they have enjoyed and raised their children in can be passed along through our process to a deserving family who will be raising their family there, while helping the community as well.

Whether you are a buyer, seller, lender, or real estate investor, you can likely see how it makes perfect sense to work with - and be inspired by - a Certified Affordable Housing Provider® offering the *Path To Home Ownership*® program.

Join me now and become inspired by people from throughout this country who are changing lives and making a difference in the world by 'Doing Good While Doing Well' ™.

Doing Good While Doing Well

About Lou Brown

Investors have long regarded the training, systems and forms created by **Louis "Lou" Brown** as the best in the industry. Quoted as an expert by many publications such as *The Wall Street Journal* and *Smart Money,* Lou draws from his wide and varied background as a real estate investor. Having bought property since 1977, he has invested in single-family homes, apartments, hotels and developed subdivisions, as well as building and renovating homes and apartments. These experiences have given him a proving ground for the most cutting edge concepts in the real estate investment industry today. He is widely known as a creative financing genius regarding his deal structuring concepts. He enjoys sharing his discoveries with others as he teaches seminars and has authored courses, books and audio training on how to make money and keep it.

Lou is past President and a lifetime member of Georgia Real Estate Investors Association and was founding President of the National Real Estate Investors Association. He firmly believes that the path to success is through ongoing education, and invests thousands of dollars annually in his own.

Lou loves to spend time in Atlanta with his beautiful wife Janice, their two children and foster daughter, and he always makes time to speak with other realtors and investors about his *Street Smart* and *Path to Homeownership* programs.

So if you are interested in learning how Lou can take you to the next level, then visit his website at **www.louisbrown.com** or contact him directly at **StreetSmartLouis@LouisBrown.com**.

Street Smart Systems, LLC

"What I hear, I forget.

What I see, I remember.

What I do, I know."

~Chinese proverb~

Chapter 2

Why They Call Him the "Warren Buffett" of Real Estate Investing
By Jeff Weiller

"Many shall be restored that now are fallen and many shall fall that now are in honor." ~ Horace-Ars Poetica

During weekly family dinners in the 1970's a family friend, mentor and early partner of Warren Buffett's would sit down with me and teach me about Value Investing. In simple terms, "Value Investing" is the strategy of selecting stocks that trade for less than their real values. Believe it or not, I always found this to be a fascinating subject, so at his suggestion I studied Benjamin Graham's textbooks, which were used by Graham to teach his Value Investing class at Columbia University. On a side-note, Columbia is where Buffett studied under Graham and received a Master's Degree in Finance.

In addition to the textbooks, I also studied Buffett's letters to partners and shareholders. A careful study of these letters is considered by many to be as valuable as an MBA from Harvard University.

Bottom line --- I was hooked and became a "Value Investing" disciple and practitioner!!!

I also learned Buffett's primary investment rule: *"Be fearful when others are greedy and greedy when others are fearful..."* and adopted it as my own.

Doing Good While Doing Well

After receiving a Master's Degree in Finance and Statistics I went on to pursue a career in Manhattan commercial real estate. During that time my Value Investing education, training and experience was applied, earning commercial real estate brokerage commissions and saving and Value Investing. My value investments consisted of buying undervalued securities and buying delinquent real estate tax sale certificates earning 18%. The delinquent real estate tax sale certificates were either paid back by the property owner or I received title to the property for 10 cents on the dollar, and quickly sold it to other real estate investors for 40-50 cents on the dollar.

Way back in 1992, a time very much like today, I found myself in the depths of a recession and real estate depression. These economic events were triggered by real estate investing tax reforms, the 1987 stock market crash and oil price spikes. At that time, through the application of Napoleon Hill's *'Principles of Success'* I was able to close and collect quite a large commission on a major office space leasing deal. Taking what I had learned, I decided to invest my commission in Buffett's company 'Berkshire Hathaway,' which I felt was highly undervalued at the time. I was able to purchase shares at $4,800 and sold them some six years later for $78,000 a share, a compound annual return of approximately 59% per year. Not bad for a rookie!

Following the tragic events of 9-11 I worked with business leaders in the restricted zone of the World Trade Center to relocate their businesses. Even though this was a very rewarding job, my personal goal was to stop commuting 3.5 hours roundtrip a day from CT to NYC and spend more time with my family while working from my own company closer to home.

My business goal was to further apply Value Investing to real estate during the real estate crash that I was able to see coming. So I started my own value oriented investing business while going to school part time to earn an MBA in Value Investing from Columbia University. There I was lucky enough to study under many of the top value investors of our time.

During the interim I was able to partner with Louis Brown, one of the Godfathers' of Value Oriented Real Estate Investment. The Great Recession, which began in 2008 and seems to be "scraping along the bottom," has provided Value Oriented real estate investors with some fantastic opportunities.

My Great Discovery

Along the way I learned that I could apply the same time tested principles of Value Oriented stock market investing to real estate. Now you may be saying to yourself, "Okay. Warren Buffett got rich and made his investors rich by investing in the stock market and companies, but how does that apply to real estate?" Well, Buffett and other practitioners of Value Oriented Investing buy businesses and stocks at big discounts to intrinsic value with a margin of safety for unforeseen events. Stocks are just part ownership in those businesses.

Investment real estate is simply a business that can be valued and invested in just like any other business a Value Oriented investor might purchase. We've all heard the saying about stocks: Buy Low, Sell High. Isn't that what we tend to do with Real Estate? We (generally) don't buy a house for $350,000, put $150,000 in rehab costs into it, then turn around and sell it for $289,000. We hold it until we can either recoup the money we put into it, or sell it at a higher price so that we can reap the dividends.

So you see, it doesn't really matter if you are buying stocks, a business, or real estate, because the premise of "Value Investing" still remains the same.

There are a vast number of reasons why investing in real estate is an excellent choice for growing your wealth. But let's look at my **7 Value Oriented Real Estate Investing Benefits:**

Benefit # 1: Buying real estate at a substantial discount to intrinsic value with a margin of safety for unforeseen events
Real estate investment properties are businesses that can be analyzed and valued as a business...these are available today at deep discounts to intrinsic value with good margins of safety.

Benefit # 2: Extremely Low Risk Protection and Preservation
Your three primary rules of Value Oriented Real Estate Investing: 1) Don't lose money; 2).Don't forget rule number 1; and 3) "Be fearful when others are greedy and greedy when others are fearful..."

Benefit # 3: A large income check
This and regular reporting management is handled by an expert manager.

Benefit # 4: Great returns, usually high returns
Your money doubles in size every 10 years at a 7.2% interest rate or rate of return protected by safe real estate.

Benefit # 5: Equity Buildup

At the same time you can get cash flow and build equity in your properties, which will provide a big payday when the property is sold or refinanced.

Benefit #6: Tax Free or Tax Deferred

You can invest money from your IRA or 401K into this Real Estate Tax free or Tax deferred plan, depending on the type of IRA you have.

Benefit #7: Must have professional management

Your real estate investments must be professionally managed so that you can focus on the whole picture.

So who is this NOT for? Anyone who is expecting to get rich overnight, or with no money down. This is not late night television, folks. This is Value Oriented Real Estate Investing, which can build wealth quickly through high rates of return and preservation of capital

Who Should Take A Serious Look At This? Anyone that has more "money than time" should take a serious look at this.

If you fall into one of the following categories, then you should request my free report at **www.realestatevalueinvesting.com** immediately before they are all spoken for:

- You are busy carrying on with the daily cares of life;
- You want to supercharge your IRA, Roth, Keogh or SEP. Yes, retirement funds can be invested;
- You want to be as close to pro in Value Oriented real estate investing but do not want to devote the time on

management of the investments. A true and realistic "short cut";
- You want to work side by side and have access to one of
- You want to work side by side and have access to one of the foremost experts in Value Oriented investment real estate in the US...

Doing Good While Doing Well

About Jeff Weiller

Jeff Weiller shows you how to have real estate investing done for you, based upon Warren Buffett's investment principles, with low risk and solid consistent returns.

After receiving a Master's Degree in Finance and Statistics, Mr. Weiller went on to pursue a career in Manhattan commercial real estate as follows: 1) Financing commercial real estate with GE Capital, Inc.; 2) Was mentored by two of Manhattan's top commercial real estate deal makers; 3) Became a partner with those top deal makers; and 4) Became a senior broker at CB Richard Ellis, Inc., one of the premier commercial real estate companies in the world.

To find out more about Jeff and how he can help you, visit him at:

We Buy Houses... www.nyconnrealestate.com
We Sell Houses... www.brixtonrealty.com
We Help Investors too... www.jwcapitalcompany.com
We Own & Buy Apartment Buildings:
www.realestatevalueinvesting.com/content/managementbio

"So live your life that the fear of death can never enter your heart. Trouble no one about their religion; respect others in their view, and demand that they respect yours. Love your life, perfect your life, and beautify all things in your life. Seek to make your life long and its purpose in the service of your people. Prepare a noble death song for the day when you go over the great divide.

Always give a word or a sign of salute when meeting or passing a friend, even a stranger, when in a lonely place. Show respect to all people and grovel to none.

When you arise in the morning give thanks for the food and for the joy of living. If you see no reason for giving thanks, the fault lies only in yourself. Abuse no one and no thing, for abuse turns the wise ones to fools and robs the spirit of its vision.

When it comes your time to die, be not like those whose hearts are filled with the fear of death, so that when their time comes they weep and pray for a little more time to live their lives over again in a different way. Sing your death song and die like a hero going home."

~ Chief Tecumseh ~

Chapter 3

Flipping Is Back
By Laura R. Abbott

*"A good head and a good heart are
always a formidable combination."* ~ Nelson Mandela

Ever since I was a little girl my dream was to be involved in real estate. My mother used to clean vacant houses for realtors, and I used to beg her to let me help her clean, just so I could see the inside of the houses. I loved exploring all of the houses, but I was especially drawn to the character of old houses. I used to run my hands across the curved banisters and take my time slowly cleaning all the nooks and crannies. Later, when I was in middle school, I used to cheerfully volunteer to accompany my mother to real estate open houses to satiate my curiosity. I knew I wanted to somehow be involved in real estate when I was older.

Right out of college I worked as a secretary in the real estate division of an investment banking firm. I was so envious of the people in the acquisitions department; they were the ones who looked like they were having the most fun. Once again I thought to myself "I want to be involved in real estate some day!" After that job, I was a legal secretary for a real estate tax attorney. A little less exciting than the previous position, but still in real estate….

At the age of 25, with my first husband, I bought my first house. Finally – I owned real estate!!!! Fortunately, my desire to be in and to own real estate lasted longer than that marriage…

Doing Good While Doing Well

Within a couple years I was remarried, and together with my new husband we bought a total fixer-upper. What a fun project that was (no sarcasm intended) – layer after layer after layer of wallpaper, paint, carpeting and tile. We were just about done with the whole renovation when we received an offer that we just couldn't refuse. We sold that place for a nice little profit and found our next home – another fixer upper. This one had been vacant for over a year, replete with cobwebs and dead bugs in every room, but I could see myself standing in the kitchen with an apron on, so we called the beautiful Tudor "Home." After five years, it was time to move again, uprooting the family from Chicago's suburbs all the way to White Plains, NY.

We were so incredibly fortunate to be able to purchase a very large colonial money pit (sarcasm intended), pouring a ton of money into bringing this grand dame to her previous grandeur. During our five years in this wonderful home, I redid the living room, the dining room, the bedrooms and some bathrooms, painstakingly choosing colors and fabrics. But a looming divorce caused yet another relocation. I swear my ex-husband tried to break me with my post-divorce house which he was allowed to help me choose. I spent a lot of money on red wine and boxes of tissues as I repaired four simultaneously leaking bathrooms (and also renovating two of them), a kitchen without heat, a couple of decks, landscaping, water in the basement and a leaky roof. A screw through a thumbnail, a tetanus shot and subsequent chelation therapy for lead poisoning did not deter me. I made this house shine; she was beautiful! But then I got news I was not prepared for. Just before our divorce was final, my ex informed me "I'm buying the house 2 doors down." NOOOOOOO!!!!

But now was my time to do what I had really wanted to do for so long. I once again sold the family house. But this time I identified two houses in a package deal – one to rehab and to live in, the other to rehab and put tenants in. I did it! I finally became a landlord and started collecting passive income! I carefully screened my tenants and found fantastic people to live in the house that I had lovingly renovated, giving the new residents a beautiful place to call home.

During the last few years that I had been living at the last house, I had begun studying real estate, attending courses and reading a lot of books. I wanted to prepare myself for a career in real estate investing. While I renovated my present house for my family and myself to live in, I also found another local house to buy and renovate, but I didn't have enough money. I had to find someone willing to lend me $200,000. Wouldn't you know it? Luck, determination, an impeccable reputation and persistence were on my side and I was able to find someone to entrust me with their investment dollars. I was now able to fix and flip my first property for a tidy little profit.

I was hooked!

The next year I renovated a few more houses and wholesaled some others. I continued to educate myself and to attract additional private individuals who wanted to earn higher interest rates on their investment dollars than they were currently earning in their IRA's and/or money market accounts to invest in my projects. What incredible fortune when I was offered the opportunity to be interviewed on CNN (see "Flipping is Back" so you can hear me say "Cha-ching" on air. Yes, I really said that....) This exposure helped me to attract even more private lenders.

Lessons Learned

Many important lessons were learned on-site that couldn't be taught in the classroom: choose partners very carefully, don't be afraid to ask questions, don't be afraid to walk away from a deal, and – most importantly – trust your gut! Oh, and don't climb onto kitchen counters in short skirts and high heels...

Over the years I learned the importance of getting the appropriate education, of having mentors and coaches and of surrounding myself with a community of like-minded individuals to support me. It's not easy to move forward with your dreams when other people doubt you and pull you down by the ankles and tell you "you don't know what you're doing" or "you'll never make it." But four years later, I have done many real estate deals, raised over $1 Million and even experienced some of those wild "No Money Down" deals you don't think are real until they happen to you.

Over the past year I have taken the time to sit back and reevaluate my business: What exactly am I doing and why am I doing it? When I shifted my attention from myself to my customers, my business took off. When I focused on earning higher returns for my lenders and also on providing opportunities for tenant/buyers that they couldn't find elsewhere, everything fell into place. I quit focusing on the bottom line (without having lost sight of it) and began finding ways to add value to others.

One of my favorite real estate transactions was when I found a couple wanting to sell their home on their own because they couldn't afford to pay a realtor. We were about to sign the contract when another person, a renter, entered the picture. The couple ended up renting the house to the tenant instead of me.

However, I followed up with the sellers for over a year, just checking in on them to see how everything was working out for them, being landlords from across the country and all. After a year, the husband emailed me and said "Help me, Grandma! I don't want to be a landlord." I got into contract with him shortly after that and solved his problem. I then found a lovely young woman with bad credit who could not qualify for a bank loan, even though she had a nice chunk of change to put down. This same house was perfect for her! She was so incredibly happy and grateful to have found a house to call her own and to not have to qualify for a bank loan. This type of transaction, helping sellers and helping buyers, is what makes my business successful and gives me joy.

Here's another example of how being a real estate entrepreneur has allowed me to help another person. A female tenant/buyer I am currently working with left her previous home and an entire state to get away from an abusive husband. She is apprehensive to buy a house in her own name for fear that he could find her again. Through my real estate training I possess the tools to be able to help her and keep her name out of public records. To the average reader, this may seem like a tiny gesture, hardly worth a mention in a book. But to this woman, and to others in her position, it could be the difference between life and death, and I am so happy to be able to provide a solution.

Besides helping tenants and buyers, helping my private lenders earn a higher rate of return gives me great satisfaction, too. A man once invested a considerable amount of money with me and was happy with his return. After his capital and interest were returned to him he decided to try his hand at rehabbing a property. He was lured by the promise of a greater return by another rehabber who wanted to create a joint venture. Unfortunately, neither of the men knew what they were doing and after over 15 months, this gentleman's expected 30% return turned into the same return that I would have given him -- without the risk. Shortly after that transaction, the gentleman returned to me and invested even more money than he had before. Having private lenders who do multiple investments with me is a testimony to their trust in me, in my business and in real estate.

Just Say Y.E.S.

One of the advantages that working for myself has afforded me is to create my own schedule. As an adjunct to what I do in real estate, and through training I received through the self-development company called Landmark, I am so fortunate to be spearheading a program called Y.E.S. (Young Entrepreneurial Spirits) in which I am teaching entrepreneurialism to high school students. I get such a thrill from talking to these young, creative minds about owning their own businesses some day and from introducing them to entrepreneurs from various walks of life. They're hearing from other generous entrepreneurs about the qualities it takes to be a successful entrepreneur, the paths that they each took, sage advice, and about benefits and pitfalls of working for one's self. By the end of this year they will have benefited from hearing from an insurance company owner, a restaurateur, an IT company owner, a real estate entrepreneur, a chocolate purveyor, a man in the textile industry, a French boutique owner, and so many more.

This Y.E.S. team has learned the importance of being impeccable in their word, of being punctual, of pursuing their dreams, of surrounding themselves with other positive people. They've been made aware of continually taking steps towards their goals, of reading or listening to inspiration material, of having fun.

My hope is that these young people will have been permanently inspired to become entrepreneurs themselves one day and be able to give back to future generations themselves.

And maybe even a few of them will find inspiration from my story and join me on the journey of helping others with their dreams of home ownership.

Doing Good While Doing Well

About Laura Abbott, CAHP, CTS

Laura Abbott is the busy, divorced mother of five and grandmother of one originally from NW Indiana but currently living in White Plains NY. Before becoming a real estate investor, Ms. Abbott had received a Bachelor's Degree from Indiana University – Bloomington and then worked as a legal/executive secretary and office manager in Chicago. She quit her last "job" almost overnight when she adopted two nieces in 1990, married and became a stay-at-home mom while subsequently adding three biological children to the family.

After years of carpooling, PTA, fundraising, Brownies and Girl Scouts, coaching/managing Little League teams, tutoring English as a Second Language, housing foreign exchange students, renovating her family's various homes after each move, being a Court-Appointed Special Advocate, she and her husband divorced. Ms. Abbott decided that it was time to try her hand at real estate. She first obtained a real estate salesperson license, and then she invested in her real estate education by taking seminars/courses in short sales, buying, selling, land lording, 1031 tax exchanges, apartment buying, trusts, lease options, business management, negotiations, renovations and accounting for real estate investors. She also became a Certified Affordable Housing Provider (CAHP) through Lou Brown and his Street Smart real estate system based in Tucker, GA.

When not involved in her real estate business or with her children, she can be found learning new things, skeet shooting, archery, travel, meeting new people, self-improvement courses and hopefully golf in 2014!

Also:

- Inaugural class of White Plains Citizens' Police Academy
- Member, White Plains Public Safety Advisory Board
- Member CTREIA
- Recipient of The 2013 Connecticut Women in Real Estate Award

Ms. Abbott can be reached at Laura@ApplePieProperties.com and through her websites:

www.GrandmaSellsHouses.com

www.GrandmaBuysHouses.com

www.GraniteReserves.com

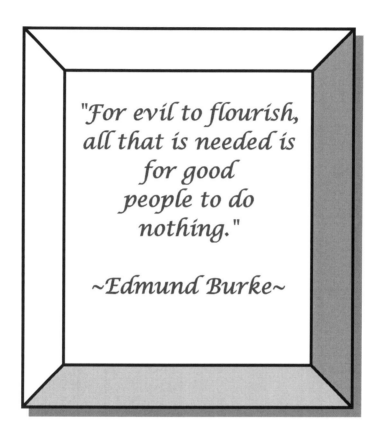

"For evil to flourish,
all that is needed is
for good
people to do
nothing."

~Edmund Burke~

Chapter 4

Making Money While Making a Difference
By Edward & Suzanne Lackey

"We Transform Lives Through Affordable Housing to Empower Families and Individuals to Enjoy the American Dream of Homeownership"

We'd like to share something wonderful with you. In 2011 we were fortunate to meet Lou Brown, and because of this meeting we have become Certified Affordable Housing Providers. Since becoming a CAHP member, we have received much more than money from the services that we provide. In this chapter we would like to take this opportunity to explain how Lou's programs have helped make a difference in not only our lives, but in the many lives that we have been able to help.

Through our *Path to Home Ownership Program*, we are making a difference in people's lives. By giving people the opportunity to buy a home, instead of just renting, their sense of self-worth rises. They now take more pride in themselves, as well as their home. We have had families with tears in their eyes, (as well as ours), when they realize that they are buying their Home. The CAHP Program is also making a difference in the community. We buy vacant houses and together with the home owners rehab and revive the community. We have noticed that when people are buying their own home they are more apt to make improvements to their home by painting, decorating, and so on. They also make landscaping improvements to their yards, which makes a difference in the appearance of the community.

Our *Work for Equity* program has helped to fill our homes with little or no repairs by us. Some of our clients are able to get into a home with very little down payment. We market the homes to be rehabbed by us, but if the home owner does not have enough money down, we are able to offer a discount on their down payment if they do some or all of the repairs. In the past we would rehab the home to our taste, only to find out that the home owner would like to paint the house a different color, change from carpet to wood flooring, have maple cabinets instead of oak, etc. By having the buyer choose their preferences, or even supplying their own paint, we are no longer repainting, which saves us both the labor and paint costs.

This is the only way for most of our clients to buy a home because their major concerns are with the down payment amount, as well as the monthly payment. By putting people on the *Path to Home Ownership* program, we not only avoid them comparing our price to another home for sale, but the majority of the time we are able to get the full asking price of the home.

We are also making a difference in the home seller's lives. We are able to buy their home NOW so that they can move on with their lives. There is a vast amount of people who have their home on the market for months, or even years, and we are able to immediately buy their home, subject to existing financing. This allows them to move on with their plans and goals, instead of the home holding them hostage.

In some cases we are even able to pay cash for the homes at a discounted price. Lou has graciously showed us how to raise private funds for this. (Lou has never gone to the bank to finance a single family home!) Through our bank we have also been able to set up a line of credit to buy these homes. We buy the homes for cash, rehab them and put qualified homeowners in them. We then show the bank that they "cash flow." Showing a positive cash flow allows us to get bank financing on them so that we are then able to pull out all of our investment capital to use for the next house. We have done this process over and over again with several homes being done at the same time. We currently use 3 separate banks for financing the homes. We purchase some of the homes from these same banks with no competition. They do not want to end up with houses that need repairs upon repairs, so this is a win-win for both the bank and us. We are able to buy the home at a discounted price, and the bank gets the home off their books faster.

Now by using *The House Monster* we have cut down on our vacancies and holding time. *The House Monster* helped us create a buyers list. On this list we have information from our buyers such as: how many bedrooms they need, location they are interested in, price range they are comfortable with, etc. So when we acquire a new home we put it out to our buyers, and many times this presents us with multiple people interested in the home. Many of our houses are filled within one week of purchase because we start advertising once we put the house under contract. Sometimes we are even able to show and hold open houses on a home even before we close.

I also like to apply to the theory of "Always Be Marketing." Even if you do not yet have an available house, you should still be marketing the program. Sometimes I look for houses to buy in a high traffic area just to help market the program.

We also have a VIP Program, where people can put money down until we find them a home. This works well for both our clients and us. They are able to start saving up the down payment, and we know that they are serious about buying.

Being a Certified Affordable Housing Provider also allows us to connect with other CAHP's across the country. We are challenging, praising and helping each other on a daily basis. If we are having a problem we can put it out to other CAHP's who are always willing to help work through it. We all come from different parts of the country and different backgrounds, so we are able to see things from different angles.

Lou has not only taught us how to buy, sell, and lease real estate, he also has the best asset protection program in the country. Using his *Maximum Asset Shield* program we have learned how to do estate planning to protect our assets and pass them on to our heirs.

In closing, using the tools, training and coaching from Lou Brown and his fantastic team has truly transformed the lives of not only our clients, but ours as well.

Doing Good While Doing Well

About Edward & Suzanne Lackey

Edward and Suzanne Lackey are active real estate investors who have bought and sold hundreds of properties. They started investing in Real Estate in 1996 building new homes. The expansion of their business led them in the direction of acquiring and rehabbing homes that they make available for the Certified Affordable Housing Provider program. Together they have over 20 years in the Construction and Real Estate business. They both are actively involved in several Real Estate Investors Groups in the St Louis, MO area, which keeps them up to date on the swings in the market.

They have expanded their market through the CAHP program to give individuals and families the opportunity to follow the American Dream of Home Ownership in Missouri. "This program has opened the doors for Home Ownership to people who could not get into a home of their own through the normal lending process. It is a wonderful experience to see the smiles and hear the "Thank You's" we get when placing people in our homes. It is a WIN- WIN for all involved," says Suzanne Lackey.

The Lackey Group, LLC is a multi-service company. They buy, sell, lease and owner finance property.

Wanting to buy a home? Contact them at their website at **www.affordablehomesellers.com.**

Needing to sell a home? Contact them at their website at **www.tlghomebuyers.com.**

You can also contact them directly at 636-744-1255, or visit them at their office at: 307 South McKinley Ave. Union, MO 63084.

Chapter 5

The Best Investment of Your Life
By Danny Schayes and Wendy Lucero-Schayes

"Learn from other people's mistakes; you don't have time to make them all yourself!"~ Winston Churchill

Who really are the most successful people in the world? (The answer WILL surprise you!) How can I use their system to help me be successful also? What are the real keys to success that I can actually use in my life to achieve my dreams?

While Bill Gates, Richard Branson, and Donald Trump are a few of the richest people in the world, their unbelievable success was the result of unique circumstances. The key factors that made them business titans are not reproducible by the vast majority of real people. While their stories are fascinating, they are not very useful as far as practical business models.

So what is the most understandable, most proven, and practical success model ever created? Which is the model that you can use to achieve real lasting success? Which model is successfully used by millions of people each year to reach their goals and maximize their potential?

It is the model that athletes use to achieve greatness!

(Surprised?)

So how do we know the answer? We've lived it for 40 years and have seen it in action with thousands of people on every level........from beginner to Hall of Famer.

For me, the key to my success was learning from a variety of many different coaching styles and bringing that knowledge onto the court. As an older player my experience was a real benefit that I used on the court and shared in the locker room. The value of excellent coaching showed up in extending my career by several years. That equaled quite a bit of money that still pays dividends as my career continues as an analyst/reporter and coach. For me, the great coaching that I received will benefit me for the rest of my life!

When our competing careers finally ended, mine as a professional player for the NBA, and Wendy as a National Champion and one of the top 2 female divers in the world, the value of coaching was still apparent.

Now retirement from sports is not quite the same as retiring from a traditional job. The first big difference is that in sports you are done between 30 and 40 years of age. You are way too young to go out to pasture, but at that age you don't fit into the typical path of career advancement.

We found out the hard way that we had to make our own way. We both retired from professional sports and figured out pretty quickly that we were lost. Wendy's Olympic career ended when she was 29 and my basketball career ended a little later at 40. We immediately realized that we had a big problem. How could we enter the job market competing against 20 year olds starting out? We didn't possess the business skills that folks our age had default. We were unemployable!

Doing Good While Doing Well

We had college degrees and the benefit of money in the bank to start with. Yet there was a big hole to fill to find passion and purpose. We needed to make a living and have a reason to get excited about being productive every day.

Thus began the quest to see what we wanted to be when we grew up! We started by taking seminars on different topics. We studied real estate investing, stock trading, personal development, asset protection, tax strategy, and others. We searched out the leading educators and got to know each one as we went along. We found tons of specific "how to" information out there. We were looking to see what we were best suited for and what we would excel at. But we still struggled on where to start.

Athletes learn in a system. In life after basketball and the Olympics, that system didn't exist. So we backed up and started learning about how successful business people operated. It became apparent to us pretty quickly that we weren't going to operate like Bill Gates, Warren Buffet, Donald Trump, Richard Branson, or any of the other folks out there with billions of dollars and thousands of employees. Their stories were not very helpful in that regard.

So we kept looking. Finally one day the answer hit us like it fell out of the sky. We were already masters of the most proven success model ever created.... ***how to succeed in professional sports!*** We immediately started breaking down the elements that athletes use to be champions. What we detailed was the most understandable, easy to follow, and effective system that we have ever seen.

There are several distinctions athletes do better than everyone else and are at the very foundation of consistent achievement. We will go over one of the key success elements that help separate sports from other endeavors. It is one thing that sports people understand and use more than any other industry.

The Value of Great Coaching

Athletes view coaching as such an important part of their success that virtually ALL ATHLETES on every level have one or more coaches AT ALL TIMES! It is not only in team sports, either. Individual athletes on the highest level, whether it be Tiger Woods, Usain Bolt, Michael Phelps or Serena Williams have not only one, but teams of coaches.

Athletes will have a professional coach, a strength coach, a sports psychologist, and a health coach among others. They never play without a coach. Team athletes have even more layers of coaches. It is not unusual for a top team to have a head coach, one or more assistant coaches, position coaches, and others. Individual players often employ their own specialty coaches, like a shot coach, a pitching coach, or some other specialized coach.

What is interesting to note is that the higher the level a player attains, THE MORE COACHING IS INVOLVED! You would think that as a player makes it to the pro level he has it all figured out and needs less coaching. Not so. Athletes understand better than most people that great coaching more than pays for itself. It makes them *more money*.

It's obvious that athletes make their living directly from their performance, so coaching is a natural investment. So what about other areas of business and entrepreneurship? Isn't the key to success long hours and hard work? Does coaching matter for them?

Let's look at the value provided by great coaching and see if it sounds like something that an entrepreneur would benefit from:

1. **Leverage other's knowledge and expertise**
   The first reason that you get a coach is to learn from someone who knows more about what you are studying than you do. This access will save you years of learning time by teaching you the specialized knowledge you need to succeed.

2. **Leverage other's experience**
   Once you learn the specific information and start taking action, it is typical to get stuck by all of the things that happen in real life that aren't in the textbook. Why spend years making expensive mistake after expensive mistake when you can have an advisor guide you through the landmines that you will face?

3. **Provides accountability**
   One of the hardest things to manage in life is distractions. When starting a new business, it is typical to keep doing what you have been doing while you transition. Before you know it, days of inaction turn into weeks and nothing gets done. A coach is really useful to keep you on track with milestones and appointments, providing deadlines to keep. This function is one of the best indicators of success.

4. **Provides structure and resources**
   Most entrepreneurs start businesses on a small budget, doing most of the work themselves. They feel the need to save money by taking on more jobs. Or they may need specialty help that they don't know how to find. Buying

and selling real estate needs a variety of people, such as: contractors, marketing people, bookkeeping and accounting services, etc. A good coach can provide these folks from their own network, or teach you how to screen people, helping eliminate the waste and losses from bad hires.

5. **Can see things hidden from you**

   One of the most unappreciated elements of coaching is the outsider's perspective. The reality is that you only see what you can see. If you have a blind spot, nothing in the world will help you see it on your own. We all get tripped up by our own perspective and rationalizations. It's amazing how the things most hidden from us can be seen instantly by someone else. That's why there is a huge value in being able to bounce ideas off someone else.

6. **Provide inspiration**

   Sometimes it's the simple things that make a huge difference. In every business there is a point after the fun wears off, but before the money is rolling in, that we just have to put one foot in front of the other and soldier on. These low points happen in every business, and often are enough to shut you completely down. It is crucial to have that voice urging you on, providing that push that you need. Every athlete knows that he can push through obstacles better with someone cheering him on.

7. **Support system**

   There is also a point where you will have a complete breakdown. You know enough to operate when things are working right, but you will eventually hit a spot where the wheels fall off. You have a problem that you have no idea how to solve. You're in over your head; you wiped out your bank account, lost a must-have client, or suffered some other catastrophe. You are ready to cash in your chips and bail. Without a support system you will probably give up on your dreams, efforts, and results from all of your work and investment. You need that backstop to be there and not let you quit.

8. **Helps you to overcome fear**

If you are not terrified during the process of going on your own, then you are not trying hard enough! You will be in the zone of discomfort every day, and the voice of fear is never far away. Remember that courage is not the absence of fear but the ability of taking action in the face of fear. Having the knowledge that there is someone urging you on at every turn and providing needed assistance during times of a breakdown makes the difference between success and failure.

Remember that information is cheap, and possession of it is a poor indicator of future success. The factors that make or break your success are related to your absolute commitment to making it work. That commitment is the entry fee to success. You can't be successful without commitment, but having commitment alone does not guarantee success. The benefits of coaching increase your odds immeasurably. We feel confident saying that without quality coaching you will have very little chance at success. There are just too many places for things to go bad, too many obstacles and too many missed opportunities. Coaching is the key to overcoming all of those obstacles.

We don't know of one successful person in sports or business who said "I did it all myself." That is why when athletes make more money, they invest in more coaching. The more complex the situation, the more value a coach provides.

Entrepreneurs usually think of coaching as a luxury to add as they start getting results. They don't take into account all of the results they lost by not having quality coaching. We believe in studying people who have already had similar success that you are trying to achieve. So stop trying to be Bill Gates or Warren Buffet. You have much more in common with your favorite athlete.

- He started by learning a skill that he didn't know how to do yet
- He practiced before he played
- He started small and worked his way up. LeBron James' first game wasn't the NBA Finals
- Most importantly, he was coached every step of the way

Professional athletes use a system to achieve greatness. Now you can, too!

The Next Step

When we started investing, we knew that we had to follow the steps above. Our first step was to figure out what we wanted to focus on. We learned the content at seminars, but used coaching to take action. We started in real estate buying and selling single-family homes. We started with our team first, and then built our business processes. It was important to get complete buy-in from everyone before starting.

In the process of learning at seminars we met a guy who had been flipping houses for several years and was starting out teaching at his own events. He agreed to coach us through the rough spots.

When we found our first deal, we ran the details and the offer we wanted to make by him. He also sat down with us and did a dry run so we could practice what to say. And what a good thing that we did. In the process of discussing the deal, he made us realize that we were in fact doing a terrible deal! The best coaching advice that we got was to NOT DO IT! If we had, we would have been at risk of a big loss. We learned more from almost screwing it up than we would have had we done a good deal by accident. What a wake-up call that was.

Good coaching saved us a possible $100,000 loss the first day. With continued coaching and learning we quickly got up to speed and completed 15 successful deals the first year, making a nice profit.

What was truly interesting though is what we realized by taking a lot of seminar education. Of the 15 or so real estate "experts" that we took either seminars from or saw at someone else's event, they all learned their stuff from Lou Brown. Some of the teachers specialized in some small part of the house buying and selling process, while others were professional seminar speakers who picked real estate as a topic to teach. But without exception, all roads led back to Lou.

As we mentioned earlier, when athletes become more successful they increase their level of coaching, not lower it. We soon realized that the best coach with the best teaching material was Lou Brown. Not surprisingly, he also has made a tremendous commitment to his business and practices what he preaches. Once we realized that, it was a simple choice to have Lou be our primary source of information about the business. Even today, 10 years later, we still attend Lou Brown events, use his materials daily, and stay in contact getting our coaching from Lou.

Quality coaching is a critical element to being successful at whatever you do, whether it's sports, real estate, business, relationships, or even your health. Finding the best coach for you can be a difficult process, especially as you start out.

We learned a tremendous amount from each one of our coaches, even the "bad" ones. One of the key responsibilities for a coach is to build a players confidence. Sometimes it takes encouragement, sometimes a kick in the pants! When you have a choice, picking a coach with the appropriate style is crucial. In team sports you rarely get to choose your team coach. You often get what you get and deal with it. As an individual athlete, you have a lot more control over that.

We "kissed a lot of frogs" before we met Lou Brown as our real estate coach and advisor. But the effort is worth it. Great coaching may be the best investment that you will ever make!

Doing Good While Doing Well

About Danny Schayes and Wendy Lucero-Schayes

Danny's Story

Professional basketball is **Danny's** families' business. His father, Dolph Schayes, is one of the NBA's pioneer stars. He played for a then record 16 seasons and has won every award and honor that there is, including being honored as one of the Top 50 players of all time. Danny grew up in a basketball candy store. His dad started the second basketball camp in America so he received excellent coaching as a kid. Danny was an NBA ball boy when he was 10 years old and got to watch practices and games being around the best professional coaches. Danny also played in the NBA for 18 years and has trained with 3 Hall of Fame coaches and 7 NBA Coaches of the Year.

After retiring from basketball Danny became a successful Real Estate investor. He and Wendy started small flipping single-family homes. With great coaching and experience they moved up to larger projects including developing a residential subdivision in Denver, Colorado, as well as buying and selling apartments, and raising equity for large condominium conversion projects around the country. In all, they have bought, developed, and sold over 1,000 residential units.

Danny is also a sought after speaker and coach. He currently spends time teaching life skills through basketball. He also is a media personality, having been a Rock DJ and TV color analyst. He currently is a basketball analyst, having worked for several NBA teams, ESPN, Turner Sports, and TK99 Radio covering Syracuse University basketball.

Wendy's Story

It was 8 months before the Olympic Trials and things were not going very well. Wendy was an NCAA Diving Champion and was now training with the most decorated Olympic coach in the country. For some reason, she was getting worse, not better. Her mother, who was battling advanced cancer at the time, saw that she was really struggling. Her new coach was trying to change her diving style a year before the Olympics. While the USA had dominated the sports for 100 years, the Chinese were starting to win using a robotic style of diving. Her coach wanted Wendy to change to their style, which just didn't work for her. Deep down Wendy felt that her coach didn't have confidence in her and wanted to change her into something that she wasn't. He finally yelled to her in front of the team as she finished a dive. He said, "You will never make it!"

Things got so bad that Wendy was about to quit the sport after years of dedicated work. She tried everything, but just ended up feeling lost. After she regrouped she called another top coach with an outstanding reputation and years of Olympic experience.

Wendy's new coach, Dick Kimball, was a perfect fit. He valued her style and instead of trying to change it, showed her how to make her diving even better. He was encouraging instead of abrasive. He was supremely dedicated, hardworking, and dependable. Most importantly, he knew what Wendy needed to do to win. In the remaining 8 months Wendy dove better and better, and when the Olympic Trials came around was at her peak, brimming with enough confidence to make the Olympic team by less than a point in a thousand-point meet!

Wendy was able to learn that while she was the one making the dives, great coaching made the difference between winning and losing.

Danny and Wendy now reside in Arizona with their son Logan, and have taken their knowledge of coaching to help them in the Real Estate game. To learn more about how Danny and Wendy can put you on a winning team, check them out at **www.DannySchayes.com.**

"You cannot help the poor by destroying the rich. You cannot strengthen the weak by weakening the strong. You cannot bring about prosperity by discouraging thrift. You cannot lift the wage earner up by pulling the wage payer down. You cannot further the brotherhood of man by inciting class hatred. You cannot build character and courage by taking away people's initiative and independence. You cannot help people permanently by doing for them, what they could and should do for themselves."

~Abraham Lincoln~

Chapter 6

Starting Out? Starting Over? Start with Shelly!
By Shelly Fonner

"You can't be Pitiful and Powerful at the same time!"
~ Joyce Meyer ~

I started my real estate investing career as a single Mom – wanting really hard to change where I was and where I was headed. Coming from a family of 'workers' in their same industry for 40+ years, there sure wasn't a support system backing my decision to become an entrepreneur. As I was raised by my Mom (her and Dad divorced when I was 3), I watched the many struggles my family would go through. Even though they were gainfully employed most of the year through, their wages were low and conditions painful to watch as they aged. In my young eyes I felt they were treated unfairly, unjust, and worked in conditions beyond what was acceptable. They were proud of their accomplishments, as it did put food on the table, but living conditions were meek, to say the least. Plus, I felt determined to change this cycle – It was up to me to be different, change things as they say... otherwise – I would fall trap to having this same lifestyle. After all, we are what we see, right? We become our environment. That is unless we take a different, less traveled road... in which I set out to do.

Making a decision to become a real estate investor is just the first step in making this happen. After all – not having anyone 'close' to council you, advise you, encourage you (I could go on and on), you really start from scratch, trying to figure out not only what you want to do but HOW you are going to do what you set out to do....

(the simple task of changing your life!). I chose real estate investing for 2 reasons really: 1) I had a huge interest in real estate – from houses, floor plans, prices, and people and 2) I had read and heard that many millionaires were created from investing in real estate. This seemed to be the perfect combo to me ☺

Setting out to figure which program, teacher, 'guru', I would follow was an overwhelming process in the beginning. I would spend hours online reading about which person offered what, which 'intro' offer was appealing, what 'bonus' sessions they were giving away, and what type of testimonials they had. Do this a few times over and I promise it all runs together.

In reading the motivational books about changing your life – creating your new found freedom – becoming an entrepreneur – changing bad habits into lasting good habits, etc, (those of you that have attempted to totally transform your surroundings know exactly what I'm talking about), it's crucial that you read books that talk about how to do this. The last I checked, we don't come with an owner's manual on how to do a 180, so this is important in making these changes a reality versus just a conversation I had with myself. These books would talk about my thoughts, actions, perseverance, and commitment needed to go against the odds. The stories inside these pages would motivate me beyond the daily grind and give me hope that if they could do these things then I could, too!

The good news about real estate investing is you don't have to know everything to get started, nor will you regardless of how much reading you spend on the topic. There are so many avenues for you to explore. The important part is to find a mentor and go for it! I've always said it's an Aim, Fire, Ready (not Ready, Aim, Fire) type of situation – you can adjust as you move along! Notice I said *find a mentor* – I don't want you to skip over that part or put it on the back burner – I believe it is crucial on how quickly you will grow your business! Find a mentor and get going… you will expand, change, adapt, and explore even more once you have a foundation, but do not skip this step!

I dabbled in real estate about 10+ years ago but didn't really get off the ground much. I bought a couple houses with owner financing and went to the bank and got a loan on a couple, and then I allowed life to get all busy. My full time 'job' took over, and I had settled into the 'landlord and toilets' scenario that was not super exciting to me! You know the stories that everyone has warned you about the minute you told them you wanted to explore real estate – you will soon find that everyone has their 'horror' story about tenants. I was once told that you have headaches and moments of chaos with any J.O.B… so why not have it be your own headache and chaos and create the life you want at the same time? I realized that was a good point. During this time of struggle, I really had no guidance or mentor as I described to you above. I was doing everything the hard way: no system, no proven agenda… just buying things the traditional way and honestly, the wrong way, but I didn't even know it. This is why I am telling you that having a Mentor and someone you can follow and get advice from is going to be crucial in how well and how quickly you build your business. (Make sure this mentor or guide to your business is successful and further along than you are!) Their experience can shave years off of your business growth, not to mention save you thousands!

To give you an idea to how important a mentor is to your overall success, once I found a mentor and followed their system exactly as outlined, I went from buying 3-4 homes ever to closing over 20 homes PER YEAR! I promise you, a mentor who is currently involved in the real estate industry will explode your business! The only changes to what I was doing before were having a system to follow! I didn't wake up one day with ALL the answers, I didn't get a ton of cash to buy these houses (as a matter of fact, I bought all these houses with NONE of my own money), and I was still single! I even created a busier life by adopting 4 children from the foster program while I was a foster parent. See... we can be all kinds of busy and still find a way to change our lives, our circumstances, and see our dreams unfold before us. It takes Determination, Dedication, and a Desire to make it happen! The 3 D's are what successful people talk about. If you haven't been taught these principles or maybe, like me, these things hadn't been discussed ever, then we have to educate ourselves in order to change our lives! Remember, if it were easy to change our circumstance and make our dreams come true, then every single person would be doing it! I believe it is simple, (follow the system), but it's not easy.

Keeping It In The Bank

Now that I've taken some time to explain to you where I started (to show you that if I can do it, you can do it too), I would like to talk more about the above statement I made – buying 20+ properties per year and not using my money! What would you say if I said not only did I not use MY money, I didn't use ANY money!? After all – I didn't have any money to use and I didn't know where to get the money, so I had to figure out a way to buy real estate WITHOUT money! The system in which I was following showed me how I could buy a property without money, so instead of just doing it one time, I repeated the cycle over and over again! ☺ Owner financing became a specialty of mine. This is where the owner's will carry the financing of the home (no bank qualifying) and sell to me on terms (agreement for deed or with a note/mortgage). I would market to people that had real estate to sell, but wasn't selling as fast as they needed it to sell. In other words, the property could be costing them money per month, need repairs, be sitting vacant, or maybe even have no equity, all in which was very inconvenient for them! My solution would ease their 'pain' and create a win/win/win for all parties. What I mean by this is that I would buy the home, taking the burden off their hands. I would have a property which didn't cost me any money, and I could market this home to someone as a rental, rent to own, or land contract. They would put money down or have a fee to move in with which would = profit for me! So – the seller won, the buyer (me) won, and the person moving in won! ☺

Since you will be learning so much in your new venture, your business will begin to take on different looks. There will be new vocabulary and brand new ways to increase your business right before your eyes. You get to choose - Yet another neat thing about real estate investing. If you love people, you can deal directly with them. If you decide to deal more with numbers and banks, you can do that, too. This will allow you to live a life by design, rather than by default. I also know people that start with real estate because everywhere you look, there is opportunity. But they use this as a vehicle to get the cash they need to do something else that makes them happy! The possibilities are really endless; the people you meet along your journey will empower you to move beyond your wildest expectations!

During my discovery and grow process as I call it, I realized that the system I had always used wasn't really geared toward what my business looked like today. It had been 4 years and 120 + houses with 300 transactions and I nor my business were the same as when I started. You will have these moments yourself when you begin to grow and change, and then it will be time to adapt to a new system that better fits how things are today, as well as your new knowledge!

Becoming a Certified Affordable Housing Provider provided the system and credibility to expand the property management side of the business. Having a stair step plan approach to potential clients, marketing to their ability to start at one level and move up to the next, empowering clients to have a chance at homeownership that they didn't realize they had, was a perfect partner in what we were currently doing. The credibility of the system and fellow CAHP's located around the world provided such a new angle for our business that we had not perfected. There is power in a system – in numbers – and in associations that you aren't able to accomplish on your own. Clients that are new to your business that you haven't already built a reputation with are drawn to the system and association that there are more than one of you. This helps them feel comfortable with you.

Success Stories

Offering our homes to clients that will empower them to become homeowners when they least expected they would qualify is what makes you feel good about what you do. Not only did I have a desire to change my financial situation, find a schedule of my own where I could be a Mom, and being a blessing to others really sealed the deal for me. Our clients have allowed us to not only be blessed, but be a blessing to them (that is a big deal for me – I'm not in this to be all about me!). These people and stories keep me going when I get down, have a bad week or month, become overwhelmed, and feel like giving up. I remind myself of just how important this is to them and their families as well ☺

Such as the Camp family – He is in his 40's and he and his wife had never had an opportunity to move into a home of their own with the possibility of owning it one day. He was so proud, he took the sign out of the ground and held it high and took a picture with it so he could show his Mom he 'finally' did it! Or the story of Dawn and her husband, she being on disability and he from Canada with no social security number – no one would give them a chance to move into their home much less an opportunity to own it one day – they tell us every month how they love their home! Or Betty, who had lost her husband and was living in the home all by herself for 2 years while it was listed and didn't sell. She called in a panic that she couldn't afford any repairs if something went wrong and she was literally making herself sick worrying about it. She wanted so bad to go to an apartment and rest easy at night and not worry about repairs and upkeep. We bought her property on terms (as I mentioned earlier) and she was able to use these monthly payments to pay her apartment. She was so pleased – we even helped her move! Oh yes, then there is Alvin. We had a home that needed repairs (it was actually condemned the day we bought it) and we weren't in a position to put in all of those repairs. We offered the home to him on Agreement for Deed, where he could make payments to us until paid in full. He would fix it with his own money, the way he wanted to. He was so happy; no one had ever given him that opportunity before. The home is now livable, off the condemned list, and he's made a great home for him and friends! Then there is Mikki – she needed at least 18 months before she would qualify for a traditional bank mortgage. She fell in love with one of our homes and we offered her Rent to Own (lease option) until she could qualify for the mortgage.

These are just a few of our stories that help us to feel good about what we do – about what we offer to others. We strongly feel that everyone deserves a home of their own, regardless of their past credit issues. We feel just as strongly about sellers as we do buyers. We really are here to help those that have real estate issues. As you learn and grow yourself, your tool box begins to grow as well – allowing you the different tools to use to solve their real estate issues. What you know today will most definitely not be the same tomorrow!

Increasing your dollars and helping others

The last thing I want to share with you before closing has been so exciting to us! We have been able to help many people earn more money on their investment dollars than what they were earning before! For example: Many people have 401K's or IRA's or Savings in the bank where they are earning a low 3% (or even less) on their investment dollars! Helping them to invest in real estate and increasing their rate of return (sometimes even doubling it or more!) has been fantastic! There are no tenant headaches – literally all you do is get a higher rate of return while your dollars are helping foreclosed homes; abandoned properties get fixed, repaired, and into the hands of deserving families! This is truly what it's all about … you helping your own family by having your money work harder for you – and you helping other families in the meantime. This is the true warm and fuzzies, and we love that here!

Doing Good While Doing Well

Here's what a few families had to say about this program:

> *"Shelly, I am so glad I invested my money with you. The returns are so much better than what I was getting in the bank! Thank you!"* (Tom, Los Angeles)

> *"Shelly Buys Houses! gave me the opportunity to make a lot more money on my savings without worrying it would disappear because of a bad economy. The loan was secured by real estate, so I knew I would get my money back, plus interest. What more could you ask for..... low risk, high returns, and no work on my part!"* (Carolyn, North Carolina)

I encourage all of you to educate yourself, read, and increase your knowledge with whatever you choose to do. I promise you that if I can change my life, my surroundings, all while finding my soul mate, caring for special needs children, starting from scratch... you can do this, too!! Come along with me, my friends! ☺

Increasing your Dollars while Helping Others

The last thing I want to share with you has been so exciting to us! We have been able to help many people earn more money on their investment dollars than they were earning before! For example: Many people have IRA's, 401k's, or savings in the bank where they are earning less than 2% on their investment dollars! By contrast, our lenders earn higher rates of return and they love that their dollars are used to help buy and repair foreclosed and abandoned properties, then place deserving families on the Path To Home Ownership! This is truly what it's all about ... helping your own family by having your money work harder – and helping other families, too. Working with Buyers,

Doing Good While Doing Well

Sellers and Lenders is very rewarding on so many levels! If you would like to help others while increasing your dollars earned, feel free to contact us for a FREE no obligation consultation!

Doing Good While Doing Well

About Shelly Fonner

Shelly Fonner, now married with 5 children, has been a real estate leader in Indiana since 2008. Originally dabbling in the real estate arena five years prior to this, she quickly discovered she was doing all the wrong things and had no system to follow. Only purchasing a few homes 'back in the day,' life took over and real estate didn't happen for her again until she took another serious look in 2008. Knowing how important a system was, she set out to find the missing piece in her real estate journey. Having a system to follow, Shelly was able to catapult her investing career to expand to over 100 homes and 300 transactions in just 4 short years! Eventually having her husband Frank join her in the business, this has truly turned into a 'family affair.'

When asked, Shelly's reasons for starting in real estate where not only to change her life from which she was raised, be a blessing to others, but to also have time with her kids! Shelly has one biological daughter and four adopted children and says she may or may not be done! ☺ Being a blessing to others is really what it's all about. "If I can enhance someone's life or circumstance from a piece of knowledge or skill I have, then I'm all for it!"

Someone recently spoke to Shelly about advice she had for other entrepreneurs, and she didn't hesitate to say balance was the key. She went onto say that if you are out of balance in any area of your life, then you will feel the chaos begin to unfold. When you are wearing a specific hat, she told him, 'you must be sure you are focused while pursuing a specific task,' otherwise you will spend much of your time doing things that are distracting. Social media, email, cleaning, organizing, etc., are a few things that can lead to these distractions, she said. "I recommend time management to be a valuable lesson to learn. I am always improving my time management skills," she quoted. "Be sure to schedule your time accordingly and when it is time to read, then read; or make offers, then make offers – but the problem happens when we go back and forth."

Shelly and Frank have a strong business in Indiana and are focusing on being Certified Affordable Housing Providers in their local market. Providing housing to those that cannot qualify for a traditional mortgage is extremely rewarding and provides growth in the local market. The ability to move people in and save homes from sitting vacant provides vitality within the community.

Shelly truly is a 'Rags to Riches' type of story – one that was destined to 'beat the odds!' Following Shelly through social media is one way you can follow their continued journey, and even learn tips and tricks along the way!

To learn more about Shelly, visit her at **www.ShellyBuysHouses.com**.

Chapter 7

The Win-Win Solution
By Kevin and Cynthia Shriver

*"A win-win attitude plus a win-win situation equals
a Win-Win Solution!"*

Win-Win Solutions Trust is a private Real Estate Investing Company formed in May 2007 to acquire, rehabilitate, lease or resell residential real estate. The co-managers of the company are Cynthia Shriver and Kevin Shriver, who have experience in real estate investing since 1989. The goal of the company is to provide affordable housing in Madison County, Illinois and the surrounding areas.

The mission statement of our company is *"We Transform Lives Through Affordable Housing to Empower Families and Individuals to Enjoy the American Dream of Home Ownership!"* The initial focus of the company was to acquire homes in which the homeowner was on the brink of foreclosure and offer them some credit bruising relief by negotiating a short sale with their Lender. This offered a winning scenario for the homeowner and provided inventory for the company in which the company could offer affordable housing to new or existing homeowners. As the years passed, we understood that many of our buying customers, while wanting to own their own home, had economic, employment or credit problems which kept them from qualifying for a traditional mortgage loan. Because we quickly recognized that demand, the business was expanded to include offering affordable, single-family housing to folks that might not initially qualify for traditional bank loans.

Doing Good While Doing Well

Through the Certified Affordable Housing Provider (CAHP) licensing and extensive training program, Win-Win Solutions Trust has implemented creative home purchase financing techniques such as Agreement For Deed, or Lease Purchase Agreement, which allows Customers/Buyers to make an initial down payment or option deposit while occupying the home. This allows our Customers/Buyers to make progress toward home ownership. They may even begin the home ownership process by renting the home. While living in what will eventually be their own home, our Customers/Buyers can build equity, repair their credit, establish a reputable financial management history and ultimately become qualified for a standard home mortgage. This model also gives our customers a financial incentive to maintain their properties. We even offer a work-for-equity credit, which can be used as a portion of the down payment toward the home purchase.

Through these programs Customers/Buyers will pay a down payment or option fee along with monthly payments, giving these Customers/Buyers the time and opportunity to increase their ability to secure a traditional home mortgage from a bank or other financial institution. We have also helped customers to take advantage of the down payment assistance (10% of the purchase price or $8,000 maximum) offered by the Obama administration in 2009/10. This truly helped the homeowner jump-start the down payment amount to lower their monthly payments.

Additionally, we offer to our Customer/Buyers that are in the *"Path To Home Ownership (PTHO)"* program assistance repairing their bruised credit, enabling them to be better positioned to obtain their own traditional mortgage. Having these customers fulfill the dream of home ownership, along with their improved credit, allows the local economy to flourish with their improved spending power. For these customers, the pride of home ownership enhances the stability of neighborhoods and the family unit. The PTHO program is typically a 1-3 year program with progressive incentives toward eventual home ownership via traditional lending mechanisms. While most of our customers complete the program within this time frame, we have instances of families that complete the process in as little as 6 months.

Our Customers/Buyers understand and appreciate that Win-Win Solutions Trust has demonstrated a strong commitment to parts of the community whose housing needs have been badly underserved, and where few realistic options have been available to those seeking and capable of home ownership. Win-Win Solutions Trust not only provides affordable housing, but also by the very nature of the business helps the local economy by providing work for local contractors, realtors, mortgage companies, building suppliers, and other related businesses.

We are a customer service driven business. We will go the extra mile to help homeowners to improve their credit not only by providing a credit repair service that also provides bank financing when the time is right, but additionally we dedicate extra effort to remind customers of on-time bill payments, and develop strategies with the customer to ensure it.

Being customer driven has provided *Win-Win Solutions Trust* opportunities to help individuals in unique circumstances. One such instance involved a handicapped couple who were struggling with a home payment they could no longer afford, which led them to become behind in their payments. Through our program we were able to purchase their home, freeing them of this debt, and then were able to re-sell the home to an individual that needed housing upon being released from prison. This individual wanted a fresh start in society and was not offered such an opportunity via a traditional lending path. We were able to help him own a home once again.

Win-Win Solutions Trust is able to find homes which are made available to our PTHO customers in a variety of ways. One method we employ to find homes is to help sellers that need to sell their home and have been unsuccessful via traditional marketing methods. The company also purchases homes via Estate sales or auctions where families find themselves burdened with an unwanted home from a family member. And finally, we purchase homes for the PTHO buyers as foreclosed properties being sold by HUD or a banking institution. The homes are selected for purchase based on our database of PTHO buyers and match a home based on their identified financial and physical needs for a home.

Our company uses different techniques to make affordable housing available in the marketplace. An Agreement for Deed contract is established by setting up installment payments. In the case of such a contract between a purchaser and a seller, the seller holds legal title of a property, while at the same time financing the sale price of the property to a purchaser. Up until the debt is paid in full, the Seller will hold the legal title to the property.

The fact that no deed passes hands is the primary difference between a standard deed of trust and an Agreement for Deed. A buyer can continue making payments after taking possession of the property. Remember, possession is not the same thing as ownership. Once the balance is paid in full, or earlier if the

Company decides to, we will then record the deed, thereby passing title to the buyer.

This is an alternate method of financing in a time when money is tight and qualifying for credit can be difficult, or even impossible, for many potential home-buyers. Conventional loan processing situations usually call for more processing hindrances and higher closing costs. If the buyer defaults on payments, the seller still retains all payments and clear title because he or she still retains legal title and the deed to the property.

Another Win-Win situation for both the Seller and the Buyer is that the Agreement for Deed contract benefits both the Seller and home buyer because the buyer can buy the property without having to qualify for a loan, and the Seller can hold on to the title to the property. The Buyer has all the benefits of any other home owner, including tax deductions.

The Company uses funds borrowed from private lenders to invest in real estate primarily, but not necessarily exclusively, in and around Madison County, Illinois. *Win-Win Solutions Trust* focuses on residential properties. The team makes it our business to keep an eye on business developments in the real estate markets. We believe it benefits us and our private lenders to do so, and it also helps us manage the risks of, and increases the odds of, succeeding in our investment strategy. This allows for a winning strategy for our private lenders that are afforded an opportunity to earn much higher rates of return on their money without higher risk.

Currently one of our Private Lenders has 7 different loans with us and has a goal to have at least 12 in order to receive an interest payment monthly; an interest payment for each month of the year. This lender is so confident in our CAHP / PTHO program that this has become a big part of their monthly and retirement income stream. The company also has Private Lenders that are using their IRAs and ROTH IRAs to build their retirement accounts faster with safe, higher rates of return on their money. They were looking for diversification in their investing without exposing themselves to the ups/downs of the stock market or the ridiculously low CD rates and money market funds that do not keep up with inflation. This form of investment is also appealing to elderly, retirement age individuals in that we currently have several lenders that are looking for stable, steady, fixed interest payments on their investment dollars at multiple times the interest rate currently paid by CDs and money market funds without the risk of the stock market. We feel so strong about protecting our Private Lenders' investments that we created a Private Placement Memorandum (PPM) in 2011 that was submitted to the United States Securities and Exchange Commission (SEC) per Regulation D, Rule 506 of the Securities Act of 1933, as amended. Our Private Lenders find themselves in a winning investment strategy with our program.

Win-Win Solutions Trust currently manages double-digit numbers of properties that have numerous customers on the Path to Home Ownership at a variety of levels … some have started at renting, some are Lease-Option, and others are Agreement for Deed. Members on this "Path" can begin at any level and skip levels while working toward home ownership. Moving to the next level involves increased down payment amounts, while improving their credit. These members are usually in the program from 1 to 3 years, with the ultimate goal of traditional bank financing and lowered monthly payments within that time frame.

Doing Good While Doing Well

Not only is *Win-Win Solutions Trust* in the business of helping more people become homeowners, the company also helps private lenders (individuals) earn more money on their un-invested funds and/or improve the growth of their self-directed IRAs, as well as assisting home Sellers that may need a non-traditional way in which to sell their home. As an example, we were able to help a family that wanted to sell their home. They had it for sale in the local MLS, but were unable to sell it. They needed to be closer to family members that were out of the area to help with their small children. We were able to buy their home, freeing them to move closer to their family, on a time table that met with their needs. At nearly the same time the family moved from this home, a new family, which is a member of the *Path To Home Ownership* program, moved in and is on their journey to home ownership.

In another instance, we were able to help a seller that had moved out of the home and had moved their son into the property until the son had a job transfer to Texas. The seller attempted to market the property for sale via traditional means for 8 months. The seller was fearful of damage from renting the property, so the property was vacant during this time. We were able to offer the seller an agreed upon price which allowed him to stop the monthly costs of a home that provided no source of income and that he no longer wanted. Another Win-Win solution!

There are numerous other families that we have helped avoid foreclosure by structuring short-sales with their lenders, thereby avoiding a foreclosure on their credit report. We have also been able to help some of these same people that have lost their home to a short-sale or foreclosure through our PTHO program.

Doing Good While Doing Well

The company also looks for ways in which to give back to the community with its knowledge of Real Estate transactions, mortgage lending, and insurance companies …. One such instance was involving an elderly gentleman that approached our company to purchase his home. Upon further investigation, it was found that this man owed a minimal remaining amount on his mortgage. However, he felt trapped with having to sell his home due to a leaking roof, damage from a fire, and other needed repairs, yet without the financial means to have the repairs done. In the midst of this dilemma, he was a bit behind on the small amount remaining on his mortgage. Due to this arrearage of his payments, the lender would not release the funds provided by the insurance carrier for the covered fire damage. *Win-Win Solutions Trust* coordinated with the lender to use the insurance proceeds to pay off the remaining mortgage balance and return the overage to the homeowner. We then made arrangements with a local not-for-profit organization to have the roof and fire damage repaired, and the whole interior of the home cleaned. Through these efforts, this elderly gentleman was able to stay in his now completely paid off and repaired home without any cost to him. A tremendous Win-Win solution for everyone involved.

Primary operations of our company are managed by 2 co-managers and a number of contracted businesses for specific services. Day-to-day operations include the following:

- Working with PTHO customers to match their financial and physical needs of a home
- Working with Sellers that need to sell their home
- All services associated with property management of PTHO program homes

- General contracting services for individual contractors of the following disciplines:
  - HVAC installation and servicing
  - Plumbing installation and repair
  - Electrical installation and repair
  - Flooring and ceramic tile installation
  - General carpentry
  - Painter
  - Roofing installation / repair
  - Specialists for hardwood floor restoration, plastering repair, sewer clean-out
  - Coordinated services with Credit Repair company and associated Lender for PTHO customers
- Working with new Private Lenders in order to expand the number of homes and number of families we can help
- Title company coordination
- Real Estate Agent services
- Contracting services with Certified Public Accountants
- Contracting services with Legal Counsel
- Continuing education training to offer the best of services to our customers (Sellers and Buyers), suppliers, private lenders, contractors, and the local community

In these operations, the company **Win-Win Solutions Trust** was founded and embodies on a daily basis the philosophy of always doing business with customers, suppliers, private lenders, contractors, and the community with a "Win-Win" objective.

Doing Good While Doing Well

About Kevin and Cynthia Shriver

Kevin & Cynthia were high school sweethearts growing up about 5 miles apart in rural Illinois. After graduating from separate colleges, Cynthia from University of Illinois and Kevin from Illinois State University, they married in 1982. They have been involved in real estate investing since 1989.

Both Kevin & Cynthia have had extensive training in the *Street Smart System* and have completed the requirements for Certified Trust Specialist, Certified Income Specialist, and Certified Deal Specialist. They are members of the Certified Affordable Housing Program (CAHP), as well as the Platinum coaching program for 3 years. In Jan 2012, they received the Community Affordable Housing Provider Silver Award from the GD Sanford Foundation.

To learn more about how **Win-Win Solutions Trust** can help you, visit their websites at:

www.PrettyHomeForYou.com, www.WinWinHomeSale.com

www.WinningInvestmentForYou.com

Chapter 8

Living My Dream
By Todd Warstler

"Do A Common Thing, In An Uncommon Way"
~ Booker T. Washington ~

This is one of my favorite quotes, and one of the driving forces that I live by. No one else is going to take care of me, so if I want to live life my way, then I have to be the one to better my life. This quote originally came to me from my soccer coach during my senior year in high school. It has stood the test of time, and became front and center after getting laid off about four years ago from a very successful sales career, in which I had won awards nearly every year. It was at that point that I determined that it was time to take full control of my destiny, and create my own future.

Although I majored in Finance and thought of going into real estate for a living, it ironically took getting laid off from a successful job 15 years later that propelled me into a real estate career.

Over the previous 10 years I had gotten my hands dirty renovating my own 100 year old house in Bangor, Maine. We had bought a fixer-upper that needed a lot of work. As we had time and could afford it, we went thru room by room and renovated the entire house to the way we wanted it. I also dabbled a bit in real estate during these years, but nothing serious, until I got word of the third round of layoffs coming with my employer of the last nine years. Although I had won many awards over the last nine years, I knew that I needed a backup plan, just in case I was downsized.

Aside from my wife, one of my true loves had continued to be real estate. So I decided that maybe I would become a real estate agent. Maybe this would also give me the inside track on hot deals that I could invest in!

But what I found was even better.

My future father-in-law knew of my interest in real estate and convinced me to travel to Orlando, Florida, to attend a real estate meeting. So I went to Millionaire Jump Start as his guest. That was when I was introduced to real estate investing, Lou Brown, and the *Street Smart Systems*. After this training I returned home, wanting to volunteer to be laid off so that I could get started in my new career as a real estate investor. Although it didn't happen the way it did in my mind, in the end I did end up getting downsized, thus making my decision very easy to dive into real estate fulltime.

Being conservative but very excited, I jumped into the full array of training over the next year and started working full time investing in real estate. Although it did take longer than expected, I did finally have success purchasing my first few properties, renovating them and then selling them, or renting to own them. But I did not see the returns I was seeking over that period of time, so I regretfully returned to a fulltime sales position, back on the road again for the next two years. But I had learned so much and had developed such a great team that they were able to keep things working independently, with very little involvement from me.

Doing Good While Doing Well

Through all of my training I was introduced to and became a Certified Affordable Housing Provider. It completely made sense to me. This opportunity offered me the best of all worlds! I was able to get more involved in real estate investing while helping people who wanted to buy a house, to those who earned enough, but didn't have perfect enough credit to go to a bank and qualify for a loan. On top of that, I am helping the local economy by purchasing rundown and foreclosed and vacant homes, putting people back to work fixing them up, and getting the houses rented or sold. They are generating tax revenues again for their local's communities, while helping the very people who need a first or second chance to realize their dream of home ownership! It is a great feeling to make such a difference in the lives of others. And to have such a positive impact on the community and lives of those around me. Who would have thought that I could have such a huge impact on so many!

In addition, I have also been able to help people who have lost jobs and have had to relocate elsewhere, as well as people who need to sell their homes quickly for whatever reason. Or to help people with unwanted properties, perhaps from a divorce or inheritance that they just don't want and just want to get rid of, and not have to worry about any longer.

And finally, I have been able to help the small investors, like you and I, who have money wasting away in savings accounts and CD's, often earning less than one percent, who want to increase their returns, without increasing their risks. Others have money in IRA's or invested in the stock market and don't want to ride the Wall Street roller coaster any longer, but need to keep their money growing faster than inflation. This is actually how I got started, and we can help them, too!

In many cases we have been able to increase their returns by 8 to 10 times. We also purchase properties at such a discount to the market and repair them to be very attractive homes, leaving very little potential for future housing prices to drop much further, thus providing plenty of security in their investments. And on top of that, it is in their best interest that I keep up on my payments to my investors, otherwise they would get the house if I didn't. You can't stay in business very long with a model like that! So our investors are the first ones paid.

Most recently, about a year ago, I ran off to a beach and married my high school crush. Following that, I took the opportunity to return back home to Michigan to be close to family, as well as to once again shift back into high gear being a Certified Affordable Housing Provider on a fulltime basis. And I haven't looked back! The opportunities seemed even better here, with Michigan being hit so hard with the economy and job losses, which also created a large number of foreclosed and vacant houses to choose from. I have been able to get my whole family involved in my housing business, and to hopefully create additional opportunities for them and others in the housing business.

One of the coolest things we have been doing lately as Certified Affordable Housing Providers has been the *Work For Equity* program. What makes this program so awesome is that we are now able to help people who may have more skills than cash to actually fix up a house that needs repairs that match their skills. Or they may know someone that has those skills.

This ties directly in to my theme: *"If it is to be, it is up to me."*

Doing Good While Doing Well

So this is further helping these people, who may not have enough down payment money, to fix up the house, and count those repairs towards their down payment on the house. And often times they might put in higher-end components than we would have done, and it conserves our cash from doing the repairs ourselves. And they are ultimately happier with it in the end.

There is no other better time than today to become a certified affordable housing provider! The opportunities and values out there will just blow your mind. If you desire a job where you make the decisions and work by your own rules, and create your own future and opportunities, then I don't know of a better opportunity today! And on top of that, you have the opportunity to make such a positive difference in the lives of others, as well as to help the economy by putting people back to work fixing up homes and help local businesses by buying local supplies, and best of all, to help hardworking American families to realize the American dream of home ownership!

What a difference we can make together!

And on top of all that, you have the opportunity to do this full-time or part-time as you build the business, all the while working another job or carving it out while you spend time home with the kids. And really, anyone can do it! You just need to have the desire to create a new life for yourself and enjoy real estate.

And if you are fortunate, you will even create a lifetime of residual income to provide a very bright future for you and your children, in or outside of the business. You can have the opportunity to travel the world and take some amazing trips of a lifetime!

Doing Good While Doing Well

About Todd Warstler

As a kid, I was always building something. In later childhood, I found a love for architecture and designing houses. Even to the end, where I designed my own personal island, where I designed all of the houses and businesses on the island.

4-H was another outlet for me to extend my education, learning more in-depth skills in projects in woodworking and electrical engineering. My father was always doing things around the house that he tried to keep me involved in, even though I would have rather been playing sports or watching TV.

After college, I moved to Maine and bought my first house. It was a fixer upper, with good structure, but needed a lot of cosmetic work. So over 8 years, we went through and renovated the entire house, room by room, and turned it into one of the nicest houses on our street.

At this point we started talking about the need for rental housing in my area and acquiring some apartment houses, knowing how difficult it was to find housing when we first moved to Maine. In fact, our first apartment we took sight unseen because we were moving there in just 3 weeks, and the renters were out of town that weekend, so we just needed a place to live.

So it took several years and a layoff which finally propelled me fulltime into real estate. And it was at this point that I learned about real estate investing and the potential that affordable housing had to offer.

It was the best of all worlds!

I could be my own boss, help hard working families who wanted to realize their dream of home ownership, help my local community by buying vacant and foreclosed homes up, putting people back to work fixing them up, and buying my supplies from my local vendors, who needed the revenue.

Through my additional training in real estate investing I learned multiple ways to sell the houses, including owner financing and work for equity programs, where if people have more skills than cash, they can actually do the repairs to the houses themselves, tailor them to their taste, and get credit towards the down payment on buying the house. How cool is that?

Each and every day I am expanding my business and adding more properties to help more and more people to realize their dreams of home ownership!

If you are also looking to make your dream of home-ownership a reality, please contact me directly at 866-386-0590 or check out my website at **www.NiceHomesToday.com.**

"It is not the critic who counts; not the man who points out how the strong man stumbles, or where the doer of deeds could have done them better. The credit belongs to the man who is actually in the arena, whose face is marred by dust and sweat and blood; who strives valiantly; who errs, who comes short again and again, because there is no effort without error and shortcoming; but who does actually strive to do the deeds; who knows great enthusiasms, the great devotions; who spends himself in a worthy cause; who at the best knows in the end the triumph of high achievement, and who at the worst, if he fails, at least fails while daring greatly, so that his place shall never be with those cold and timid souls who neither know victory nor defeat.

Someone who is heavily involved in a situation that requires courage, skill, or tenacity (as opposed to someone sitting on the sidelines and watching), is sometimes referred to as 'the man in the arena.'"

~Theodore Roosevelt~

Chapter 9

Welcome to the Rest of Your Life
By Johneen Davis

"I want to put a ding in the universe."
~ Steve Jobs ~

Growing up on a farm and in a small town was a very comfortable way of life. I spent countless hours dreaming of what I wanted to grow up to be and pretending what I would buy from the Sears catalog if I had the opportunity to order new clothes, instead of sewing them myself or wearing the gently used clothes from Betty's Bargain Barn. Consequently, I became a workaholic and a "study"aholic to keep myself busy and to get closer to fulfilling the dreams that I had created. My first job, other than working for my parents on the farm, was at the local nursing home where I discovered that I loved to work and care for others. At the last minute, I changed my college plans from becoming a math major to becoming a nurse.

In my first nursing program our curriculum was based on Dorthea Orem's Nursing Theory, a Self-Care Model of Nursing. One of the major assumptions was that people should be self-reliant for their own care and for the care of others in their family. When a deficit occurs, nursing action was designed to help those individuals change conditions in themselves or in their environment to restore self-care. We also learned quite a lot about Maslow Hierarchy of Needs, which is a simple stair step concept. One must first fulfill basic physiological needs such as air, food, water, and shelter before worrying about safety, love, self-esteem, and finally, self-actualization. Unfortunately, very few in our society have been able to achieve a level of self-actualization for one reason or the other. "Life" seems to get in the way and we get stuck.

My life was no different, even despite my best plans. When I became a single Mom I buried my head even deeper in work and studies, despite having previously finished a graduate degree in nursing administration, when my sons were infants and working full time as a manager in a hospital. I felt that there must be something wrong with me. I was either not working hard enough or I was not smart enough. I studied more about health care….managed care, legal nurse consulting, home care, research, and then expanded my focus to business and completed an MBA program. The problem was that I really did not have a focus. Therefore, I was having limited success. I will always thank the neighbor who gave me the advice to get my head out of the sand and get out and meet people. I found that when I started to listen to advice from others, new opportunities surfaced that I never knew could exist. I married my new husband, and have worked with two mentors professionally for the past several years who have helped me redirect my career by thinking more strategically, while still being able to care for others with my heart.

Make It Happen

"Peace on Earth Begins at Home" is a sign that now hangs over our back door entrance. It was a simple message about a home for a family that I would have taken for granted prior to divorce, a job change, a move, and prior to seeing many acquaintances face challenges in their lives that forced them to struggle to keep the basic need for shelter intact for themselves and for their families. Even when volunteering for homeless shelters in Chicago, Illinois and in Aurora, Illinois, I failed to fully understand why many did not have a place called home in America today, the land of opportunity and plenty.

Best of Times Homes, LLC, a family business, was created in January, 2013 after meeting Lou Brown and completing the *Street Smart* training program in 2012. I was thrilled to discover that a nursing background (self-care/family care) along with a business background (finance/marketing) set the stage for this next educational series, a 12 month course that included all aspects of what an entrepreneur new to the real estate world would need for success. It has been a life changing opportunity introduced to us from a networking connection here in the western suburbs of Chicago. It is important to note that the *Street Smart* team has created a very friendly atmosphere, one that was not intimidating as we participated in classroom sessions and home tours to prepare us to go out into the world to make a difference in the lives of other families. Experts in the field openly shared their successes with us, along with their cliff notes, so that we could accelerate the progress we could make, not having to recreate a system.

Doing Good While Doing Well

The mission of **Best of Times Homes** and the *Street Smart System* are congruent. Our goal is to provide families with the opportunity to live in a home and have a pathway to home ownership that might not have seemed previously possible. I have stopped being paralyzed by the fear of not being smart enough and have moved from being in the stands to being on the field and in the game.

The doors to our new vision opened before we knew it. This year, we began giving back to the community more than we ever had before. Friends have successfully been approved for loan modifications who were initially rejected but who decided to give it another try after having simple conversations with them to raise their awareness about changes in the banking industry. We helped a widow who lost her husband two years ago who was a landlord complete a transition to retirement after purchasing her properties that needed some tender, loving, care.

We helped a young family, their children, and their family dog move into an affordable home with a backyard and garage. They were uprooted twice before from homes rented from landlords who foreclosed on the properties and forced them to move, despite paying their rent on time. We shared left-over furniture with families who needed the items. We helped another family move due to a death of a loved one to then again offer an affordable housing option to the community. Our rents are slightly below market prices and we provide discounts to families who pay rent on time. We have kept our business local, already providing jobs to attorneys, title companies, accountants, plumbing and heating companies, painters, locksmiths, carpet stores, carpet cleaners, garage door repairmen, lawn services, retail stores, and garbage services.

The only thing we ask for when working with our clients is integrity. They, in turn, can expect a reciprocal relationship. Several have mentioned experiences they have had with "slumlords," which is a pretty derogatory term when referencing another party. We will uphold the city of Aurora requirements to check backgrounds and maintain a crime free community. We will educate families about recommendations we follow regarding how much they should be paying monthly for rent based on their income and outstanding debt. We will not put someone in a situation to fail, as we have seen being done over and over again.

Here are just a few notes about my lessons learned thus far...

1. **Be coachable:**
   I learned that I needed to improve my listening skills and to be more ready to act. In reality, it is one's actions that will really count. Theory is just theory, which leads me to the need to mention retirement. In theory, I have many more years to work and have time to save for retirement. In reality, time for me to save is running out, and I desperately needed to diversify my portfolio to include passive income to help retirement become sustainable.

2. **Focus:**
   I found that I was all over the map with learning opportunities in Real Estate, just as I had experienced in health care. One takeaway I received when attending my first Platinum Mastermind meeting was that I needed to focus. Unfortunately, I was not surprised, but I found that advice to be easier said than done. I needed to carefully define/design my box for properties that I would consider, consider the target service area, and utilize that 'squid

eye' developed during field training for projections. I needed to stop jumping in the car to go look at properties. I was wasting time. I had to realize that I would not be interested in all opportunities, nor could I handle them. One of Steve Jobs famous quotes that recently defined me is as follows: *"People think focus means saying yes to the thing you've got to focus on. But that's not what it means at all. It means saying no to the hundred other good ideas that there are. You have to pick carefully."*

3. **Network:**

   I underappreciated networking opportunities. Many times such events exhausted me in the past, rather than empowering me. I am beginning to see the world differently and have joined local and national real estate networking groups, along with a local running club. I have found the members of all three groups to be very inspiring, and I am looking forward to be present to new ideas and new ways of doing things and enjoying life.

Recently, one client confirmed to us that we are right on track by commenting, "We have never met anyone like you." It is an honor to uphold our promise to provide a great service to our clients.

Doing Good While Doing Well

About Johneen Davis

Johneen Davis earned a nursing diploma from Methodist Medical Center, School of Nursing, in Peoria, Illinois, a BSN and MSN at Loyola University, Chicago, IL, and an MBA at Benedictine University, Lisle, IL. Johneen works full time in the health care arena and lives in Aurora, IL with her husband Doug, who is a golf course superintendent, owner of Hawkeye Lawn Solutions, and a business partner in real estate investing. Johneen's mother, Glenda, completed the Certified Affordable Housing Provider training, too!

Life has come full circle. Some of the best of times now happen at home. They still enjoy finding bargain deals, but they are homes instead of clothes. Glenda has been able to continue to utilize sewing talents for curtains in the homes provided. Johneen thanks her parents for introducing her to hard work and teaching her to enjoy the basics. Her parents have inspired her to be an entrepreneur. They were entrepreneurs themselves in the industry of farming, something she never realized when she was living on the farm. As a family, they are looking forward to helping other families, while being able to spend more time together along the way.

Turn the page to learn more about Johneen and **Best of Times Homes, LLC**:

Telephone & Fax: 1-630-216-0050

Cell: 1-630-561-1965

www.besttimehomebuyer.com to sell

www.besttimehomeseller.com to buy

www.besttimehomeinvestor.com to invest

Our Mission is to Transform Lives through Affordable Housing and Empower Individuals and Families to Enjoy the American Dream of Home Ownership!

Chapter 10

Insulation To Inspiration
By Andrew Wendler

*"We make a living by what we get, but we make
a life by what we give." ~ Winston Churchill*

Helping people with real estate related problems was the last thing on my mind at age sixteen. I started working construction and found myself pulling insulation out of an abandoned warehouse on my first job. But, that job and the many others that followed over the next eight years would become the foundation from which I built my knowledge about residential construction, and ultimately real estate in general. In 2002 I graduated from the University of Illinois in Champaign/Urbana with a degree in marketing that provided me a well-rounded education, basic business knowledge, and very few job offers.

After graduation I moved to Texas, got a dead end job, was renting a house with a friend, was living paycheck to paycheck, and I got hooked by a late night infomercial on real estate. Even though I didn't sign up for the infomercial course, I did start looking into the business of real estate and eventually took my first class from a local organization. I was able to use this first class as a foundation to start buying & selling houses, but I had so much to learn, and I wanted to be proficient in my field. As I made a little money I continued to invest in my education, and since have attended numerous trainings from some of the best in the business; spending as much on my real estate education as was spent on my college education. In 2004 I connected with my mentor, Louis Brown, who has been in real estate since 1977 and has been quoted as being an expert in real estate, managing, and finance by "The Wall Street Journal," "Smart Money" magazine, and others. Louis's system allowed me to see the same business in a whole new way, a concept he calls "Doing good while doing well." Yes, real estate was attractive because of the possibility of making good money – but I have remained in real estate because it is possible to help good people out of bad situations. Since my beginnings in 2002, I have been part of hundreds of real estate transactions, I have seen the market grow and seen it flop, and I have seen dozens of investors go bankrupt. Through it all, I am proud to say that the companies I represent and work for have never filed bankruptcy, never lost a property to foreclosure, or even been late with a single bill or payment.

Today, I am considered a real estate problem solver, and specialize in helping sellers who have little to no equity sell their houses quickly and inexpensively. I have never come across a real estate problem there wasn't a solution for; but not every situation calls for the same solution. For example, when it comes time to sell the house, most sellers think of listing their house with a real estate agent and assume that is the only option – that it is the best option. The reality is that there are dozens of ways to sell your house, and an agent is only going to talk to you about one of them. Knowing this will help you avoid the #1 mistake sellers make:

Blindly trusting whatever the real estate agent says.

But why not, they are the professionals – right? Wrong. They are sales people that have an average life span of less than three years and they don't get paid unless they have houses to sell. Don't get me wrong, some agents are very good and some sellers should list their house with them – but not everyone. Remember three things: Question what they tell you, ask yourself if it makes sense to you, and verify the information.

<u>Tips for working with a real estate agent:</u>

A. Call multiple agencies and ask for the top agent in the office. Meet with at least two, if not three agents from different offices and ask each one three main questions:
   1. What do you think my house will sell for in the next 6 months?
   2. How long should I expect it to be on the market at that price?
   3. What repairs do you believe I need to make to have my house sell for that price and in that time frame?
B. Once you have a price that your home could sell for – run the numbers yourself:
   1. Call your mortgage company and get a payoff amount – it will be higher than your outstanding balance.
   2. Subtract the payoff from the sales price.
   3. Then deduct the costs to sell: agent, Title Company, repairs, holding costs, taxes, insurance, etc. (On average, minimum cost to sell is 12% to 20% of the sales price.)
C. Then ask yourself three questions:
   1. Based on the numbers, does it make sense for me to sell this way?
   2. Is it worth it for the amount of time it is going to take?

3. Can I afford the time and money to make the repairs recommended?

Honestly facing the answer to these questions is the most important thing you can do when considering how you are going to sell your house. If the answer to all three questions is "yes," then choose the agent you are most comfortable with and do what they recommend. If the answer to any of the three questions is "no," then read on - there is a better solution. Not being honest about the situation, and especially the financials, leads to the second biggest mistake sellers make:

Overestimating the amount of money they are going to make on the sale of the house.

This is so easy to do. Logic says you have been in the house 7 years - that's 84 payments - that's a lot of money – and now it is time to move - it's PAY DAY! Maybe/maybe not. Mortgages are amortized loans and in the early years of the loan the majority of the payment goes to interest. On average, in the first seven years only 8% to 11% of the principle will be paid off – and the average costs to sell are over 12%!! Unless there has been appreciation, most sellers are still under water after seven years. Historically, real estate does appreciate, but values dropped so drastically in 2008 that appreciation is a small factor in our current market.

When figuring the numbers, always remember:

A. To avoid emotional attachment to the monies paid to the mortgage company.
B. NOT to convince yourself the house is worth more than the agent(s) said or that the costs to sell will be less than expected.

Doing Good While Doing Well

C. **Most Importantly:** To be open to other alternatives.

Accepting the reality of the house's value and the cost to sell upfront gives a seller the ability to make the decision that is best for them and avoid going to the closing to collect a check, only to find out they have to write a check. Yes, this happens all of the time – sellers are paying out of their pockets to sell their houses. Remember, there was only 8% to 11% equity after seven years, and it takes almost 12 years to pay off 20% of the mortgage. That means anyone who has bought their house in the last 10 years are likely under water or will have very little left after all costs to sell are paid. There are thousands of people who would sell their house today, if they thought they could. The good news is, they can; just like some of these people have.

April's story goes back to 2007. She came to us on a referral from a friend. The friend was a real estate agent, and when she needed to sell their house in 2006 she came to us instead of listing the house herself, because it made financial sense. April was in her mid-30's, single, her career was not working out the way she had planned just a few years before, and she could no longer afford the house. When I met with April, I was a little surprised because her father was there also. He is a retired executive from IBM and was concerned what his daughter might be getting into. We went through the entire program together: how we were going to buy the house, and how we were going to sell the house on the *Path to Homeownership* program. Even though April was ready to accept our offer, because of her friend's recommendation, her father wanted time to think about it and to work the numbers himself. After a few days, they called back and wanted to meet again. When I sat down with them her father proceeded to tell me how impressed he was that I hadn't exaggerated the truth or stretched the numbers in our favor. That even though April would be giving up some equity, he had concluded it was a very good offer for her long-term financial future. We bought the house "as is" and gave April two months to make arrangements to move. Today the house is occupied by a married couple on the *Path to Homeownership*. They have made many improvements to the house and are excited about being homeowners because they had been denied so many times by so many other sources.

This next story is from October of 2013. Brad was selling his house because he had gone through a divorce and even though he was awarded the house, he was struggling with the payments. Not to mention the emotional connection the house had with his ex-wife. Actually, when I met with Brad he was only seven days from falling behind on his mortgage and facing foreclosure. He had been trying to sell the house "by owner" and had no luck. The house was built in the 1980's and it needed updating and repairs; money Brad didn't have. Brad had purchased the house 10 years earlier and had never missed a payment, but after we did the math together he had less than $2,000 of equity, NOT counting what it would cost to make the repairs and updates that were needed. More than anything, Brad didn't want his credit wrecked after everything else he had already been through this year. We bought Brads house and closed in less than seven days, preserved his credit, saved him the repair costs, and then leased the house back to him for three weeks for him to make arrangements to move. All for the total cost to Brad of $0.00! Brad was also happy to know he was helping to make the dream of homeownership available to someone else because his house would be part of the *Path to Homeownership* program where buyers are qualified based upon their income, and not their credit.

Doing Good While Doing Well

Tony and Janice are retired from the military and currently self-employed, but still were unable to qualify for a traditional mortgage. They moved into the house two weeks after Brad moved out on the *Path to Homeownership* and *Work for Equity* programs. Between cash and work for equity credits, they will have over a 10% down payment, are updating the house to their taste, and were able to get out of "renter ship" and into ownership. They are so happy and excited that every time I see them Janice won't let me leave until she gives me a hug.

This is why I love this business. On both ends of these examples and countless others we are helping someone the mainstream system said could not be helped. Hundreds of thousands of people have bought their house in the last ten years and would like to sell their house now, but have little to no real equity, and over 80% of Americans with good jobs cannot qualify for a traditional mortgage. We have solutions for these people. I have been able to bring First Step Management and Property Partners Group together to say YES to both buyers and sellers when the traditional real estate system says NO. The most exciting thing about what I do is being a part of making a positive impact on someone's life, helping someone see their dreams come to pass, providing a hand up and not a hand out, and making a positive impact on our community. These are things that last forever.

Doing Good While Doing Well

About Andrew Wendler

Andrew Wendler is an old fashioned American entrepreneur, real estate problem solver, a Certified Affordable Housing Provider, founder of InvestorsCoffeeHouse.com, and a Managing Partner for both First Step Management and Property Partners Group in Arlington, Texas. His career in real estate started at 16 years old as a laborer on a construction crew in northern Wisconsin. Continuing to work in construction through high school and college while today owning his own construction company, he has experienced first-hand almost every aspect of home remodeling and construction. His expansion into buying and selling houses didn't begin until after graduating from college in the spring of 2002, moving to Texas, and finding there were very few jobs available that took advantage of the business degree he had just received.

By the fall of 2002 he was working in a dead-end sales job, renting a house with a friend, and was completely broke – but, he had taken his first class on buying houses. Knowing only what he had just learned, he started looking for sellers who needed help with their house. It didn't take long and he met Curtis. Curtis had a house that he had inherited and had rented to relatives; but the relatives had stopped paying the rent, torn up the house, and created problems within the family. Curtis didn't know what to do and had no money to fix the house; he just didn't want the house or headache anymore. Since Curtis didn't need the money right away, he and Andrew entered into an owner financed agreement to give Andrew the time to make the house ready to sell and find a buyer; Curtis would then be paid his money when the house sold. Doing most of the work himself, Andrew cleaned the house, fixed what was broken, and listed the house at a discount for a quick sale. After it was all said and done, Curtis got rid of the house and the headaches, the buyer was able to purchase the house at a great value and Andrew made a profit; never using any of his own money to do it.

Since then Andrew has attended many other real estate trainings, has been part of 100's of real estate transactions, and has come to specialize in helping sellers who have little to no equity sell their houses quickly and inexpensively. Along with Louis Brown and the Certified Affordable Housing Provider program, Andrew has brought First Step Management and Property Partners Group together to help sellers out of situations that seem helpless, and then make those same houses available on the *Path to Homeownership* program to help the 80% of Americans who make good money but don't qualify for a traditional mortgage become home owners.

Today Andrew is doing what he loves, is happily married to his wife Carrie, has two beautiful daughters, and has been able to enjoy both the freedom of time and money.

If you are someone who has a real estate problem, while also looking for financial freedom, contact Andrew and his team to see how they can help you today:

Looking to be a home owner, contact:

www.FirstStepMGT.com

Needing to sell a property, contact:

www.TheHouseSolution.com

Wanting to get started in real estate and/or find deals, contact:

www.InvestorsCoffeeHouse.com

Chapter 11

Building A Community Based Business Model
By Neeld Messler

"Our customers are the most important people in our organization!"

It was 1995 and I had just gotten back from working in the deep, dark jungles of Congo Africa for National Geographic magazine. For years I had been living a transient life; roaming from one adventure to another, laying my head down wherever I ended up. This time, however, perspectives were beginning to shift for me. My draw to the caves and climbing in Chattanooga caused me to want to settle, so I decided to find a place to rent. At 25 years old, renting is what a person does. Isn't it? Or so I thought. So one particular day I was talking with my father about this and he offered me a suggestion - buy a duplex, move into one unit, and offset the monthly expense of living with rental income from the other. Really? Well, six weeks later I embarked on a new, unforeseen adventure and moved into a vacant apartment in a four unit investment property that I had just purchased. As the months passed, I came to realize that I was living not only "rent free," but also had additional income after collecting rents and paying the mortgage and expenses. This was the beginning of my real estate career.

Today I have renovated millions of dollars in real estate. Never would I have guessed that I would leave behind the action packed lifestyle of traveling the globe to become an initiator of building a community-based residential real estate company. Adopting a slow growth mentality, along with a delayed gratification philosophy, I have been able to build a real estate company that sustains the future for not only me, but for others - a "do good while doing well" business model.

The philosophy is simple – invest in residential real estate – never speculate. Investing offers a reliable and predictable return on money – buying at attractive prices in *today's* marketplace. Speculating offers a future based possibility with little reliability or predictability as to the future return on money – buying retail *requires* future appreciation. Lots of people have made fortunes from speculating. And lots of people have lost fortunes from speculating. The real estate collapse of 2008 is a perfect example. Real estate values *always* went up! America began to base the economy off of this concept. Lenders would lend with future appreciation in mind. People could buy a house and a short time later sell for a profit; or refinance the teaser introductory loans. But like musical chairs, the music eventually stops and someone gets left standing. This is part of what happened in 2008 – many were devastated.

I was one of the lucky few who was *not* devastated by the market meltdown. I prospered. This was a time of growth for my company. We were financially secure enough that we were able to buy foreclosures for 15-20 cents on the dollar. By building a business model based off of investment criteria rather than speculation criteria, I was able to weather the economic storm. When others were surviving the economy, I was flourishing in the economy and buying more houses than ever.

Since my beginning I was taught to invest at low Loan to Value. So when the recession hit, I still had equity in my properties. I could see how a few of my equities went slightly down, but they were not a loss to the business because of how I purchased. Many of my properties are cash flow dependent, and because I deal with affordable housing, and people always need a home, that income stream never got hit. We were able to manage our portfolio just like normal.

There is a saying: "think globally, act locally." I have taken this to heart through bringing real estate to a local level within my community. I have discovered that my efforts can make a difference for not just me, but also for many of the people in my community. My company helps people when they need to sell a house, as well as helping people when they are seeking a new home. My company, Home Solutions, makes a difference by offering alternative real estate opportunities for people wanting to sell, rent, or buy a home.

Today we are taking a shift in the business. I realize that we offer so much more than just homes that people can rent. Ninety percent of my real estate is long term, which in turn creates opportunity for good people to have a long term place that they can call home. Many of our tenants over the years have been college students. They get their money from their parents, they go to school, and three years later they move out. It is a solid business stream.

Three years is a long time - but what if we look beyond this? What about people wanting to have a place to call home for the *rest of their life* - people just into retirement and living on a fixed monthly income? Or people who dream of being a homeowner but do not fit traditional lending requirements? This is a lot of America!

Doing Good While Doing Well

With our long term strategy we can assist those looking to establish themselves in their new home with either our rental or home purchase program. Our company is able to provide quality, affordable housing for people looking to invest a year of their life up to their lifetime in one of our homes.

Another area where we are making a difference for people is for those looking for alternative forms of investment opportunities. Over the course of the first ten years of my career, I realized that I had paid banking institutions a <u>LOT</u> of interest money - hundreds of thousands of dollars! Contemplating this, I thought how this "profit" could be earned by someone locally – someone I know - individuals looking to grow *their* investments, for *their* life, for *their* retirement. Instead of offering this predictable, dependable, fixed-rate interest income to the banks, why not offer this to the individual?

In exploring this, I discovered there is a huge population that is in demand of this type of investment. Some people have become hesitant with stocks - realizing the tremendous opportunities, but in addition, the potential loss – and thus wanting to diversify. So why not offer these same real estate investment opportunities to people within the local community rather than the big banking institutions? This way of doing business has been able to make a difference for many local investors by offering them the exact same safe and predictable fixed-rate income investment opportunities that are collateralized by real estate.

Doctor Bill and Linda Dwyer are two investors that have chosen to take advantage of this opportunity. They were looking to grow their money in a safe and secure environment to ensure that their investments will last for their lifetime. And CDs, though safe, were not the answer because they were paying such low interest earnings. They wanted more. And this is why the opportunity worked so perfectly. They were able to more than triple their rate of return they were achieving in CD's while still having a safety net for their investment by being given a mortgage in their name against a house. Just like the banks do it. But this time *they* were the bank earning the fixed rate return while having the safety of a house backing up their investment!

Others, just like the Dwyer's have discovered this opportunity of building and securing their financial future while investing in fixed-rate, safe and secure real estate notes, while at the same time doing good for the local community and truly transforming people's lives.

At Home Solutions we are creating a winning opportunity for people when they want to invest, sell, or buy a home.

Home Solutions is the solution!

About Neeld Messler

Neeld Messler II has been active in the revitalization of properties throughout the Chattanooga, Tennessee area since 1995. Over the years he has developed a specialty in purchasing distressed properties – often times foreclosed, condemned or pending demolition - to renovate and bring back into useful and productive use. His "save what's there" vision has had the renovation impact in excess of $3 Million Dollars invested back into the community to save its current housing stock. His largest project, the 17 unit *Lofts on Main* development, has spurred the full revitalization of the Southside District in downtown Chattanooga and given a rebirth of a new Main Street for everyone. When not pursuing his passion of real estate, he has taken up the hobby of kite boarding to cater towards his adventurous spirit.

To learn more about Neeld's Home Solutions, email him at **Neeld@NoogaHomes.com,** or visit his websites at:

To Sell >>> **NoogaHomeBuyers.com**

To Buy >>> **BuyChatt.com**

To Invest >>> **FixedRateIncome.com**

Chapter 12

Real Estate: The American Dream
By Crystal A. Hill

"When I dare to be powerful - to use my strength in the service of my vision, then it becomes less and less important whether I am afraid."~ Audre Lorde

Born in New York and raised in the north end of Hartford, Connecticut, I grew up with humble beginnings. My dad was a die-hard blue collar worker and my mom had mental illnesses that would ultimately remove her from our home. I would say we were inner city middle class. My dad worked for an Aircraft company and made enough money that we didn't qualify for free school lunch. (An interesting measure of status, as I recall.) I had had aspirations of being rich from a young age. I recall a time when I would come home from school every day and use a typewriter to try to generate all of the possible combinations for the lotto. My thinking was that if I could just get up the ten thousand dollars (or so I thought) and play every combination, I would be guaranteed to win. I finally squashed that idea when I became aware of the odds and number of permutations that were involved. And then there was the comic book ad on Astral Travel. If I could only get the $12.95 it cost for that book, I could travel ahead in time and see tomorrow's newspaper today. I would play the daily numbers and my family and I would be set for life. Well, needless to say, that didn't become my reality either.

As life went on, I would discover that I was a decent student and had a propensity for math. However, I coasted through high school, opting for 101 level classes versus the honors classes I was advised to take based on placement tests. I was interested in Electronics and the Electronics class turned out to be half-year Electronics, half-year computers. Computers were new for me, and I fell in love with them. In my senior year I took as many computer/data processing classes as I could take. Towards the end of the school year, I was fortunate enough to be accepted into an accelerated program at a major insurance company where I received free computer programming training and was awarded an IT internship there. At 17, I was the youngest of 12 selected for the program. The oldest was 34 years old. The year was 1983 and I started out making 6.00/hour. Not too bad, huh? At that time, I thought for sure if I could just net $250/week, I would be set for life. LOL. Well, my pay quickly jumped to $7.10 and then $10.00, and of course, so did my aspirations. I did really well over the years, but something was still missing.

My entrepreneurial drive and spirit were in the background screaming to come out. My desire to call my own shots, become independently wealthy, live off of the interest of my money – it was still there. So I began taking a real estate course to become a realtor. I joined a couple of MLM/Network Marketing programs (you name it, I've tried it). I acquired my Series 6/63 financial licenses - all of this in an effort to figure out how to become wealthy.

And then it happened.

I read Robert Kiyosaki's *Rich Dad Poor Dad*, and life would never be the same. I knew right then and there that Real Estate investing was the answer. I joined the Connecticut Real Estate Investors Association (CTREIA) and bought just about every real estate investing course I could get my hands on. (Yes, even Carleton Sheets' from the late night infomercials!)

I partnered with a talented real estate broker and successful investor that I had met at CTREIA. Under her guidance, we successfully flipped several houses. I had become increasingly disenfranchised with Corporate America and the incessant outsourcing culture that was brewing. I decided to make my move and ventured out on my own at what is now known as the 'height of the real estate market'. I acquired a few multifamily apartment buildings and rehabbed another house. Unfortunately, during the real estate crunch I was forced to go on a bit of a Real Estate hiatus and returned to Corporate America to ride out the storm.

During this time an opportunity became available with the corporate job in an Atlanta area office. I went down to visit and decided it was time for a change. I had always been drawn to Atlanta even before I had ever been here. I found that there was so much more to do here than in Connecticut. The real estate price differential between the two states was also an attractive factor. It pained me to leave my family and friends, but I was able to work out a deal that would allow me six months before moving so I could get my family acclimated to the idea. So in December of 2011, I packed my Ford Explorer full of totes of clothes and shoes and embarked on the latest chapter of my life. I didn't really know anyone there, didn't know where I wanted to live, but I had a decent paying job and I would work the rest out when I got there.

I had decided that I was going to stay in extended stay hotels in the different cities/towns that I was interested in. This would allow me to get a better feel for the areas before making a decision. The initial town I chose was Norcross, since that was where my job was located. I soon found out that even moving simple totes around was going to be more of a hassle than I had anticipated. So, I settled in at my little extended stay spot for 6 months.

Always knowing that I was destined for greater things, I began strengthening my skills, mindset and knowledge through education. One of the most influential books that I've come across during this part of my journey has been Michael Gerber's *The E-myth*. He really has you do a self-assessment, and describes business personality types in a way that I had not considered. It was actually quite enlightening. He identified the personality types as: technicians, managers and entrepreneurs. I was able to take a personal inventory and determine that I am an entrepreneur, a visionary. Knowing who you are helps you to understand your weaknesses, so you can account for them. Mr. Gerber is also fanatical about setting up systems. He teaches that all businesses should be built from day one with a franchise-like mentality, so you can ultimately work *on* your business, not *in* your business. This was a truly amazing revelation to me.

I have always wanted to be, and help other people become successful. I believe wholeheartedly that home ownership is one of the great equalizers in our lifetime; a crucial rung on the ladder of success. I believe it instills a sense of pride, value, worth and accomplishment. It's one of those innate things, deeply rooted in the American Dream. Not to mention that it's an asset, an investment into your own, a part of the "pay yourself first" class of wealth values.

So, I pondered and toyed around with ideas. And then one day, there it was - an email from Lou Brown (*the* real estate guru) who's course I had previously purchased. But this time, it really spoke to me. He had made some changes, added some things, offered some live training sessions and done some repackaging. The end result was an extensive curriculum that would allow me to become a Certified Affordable Housing Provider (CAHP). This certification would enable me to put families on the path to home ownership in a systematized fashion, with the backing and prestige of a nationwide network of providers. I would no longer just be a real estate investor or a perceived crook out to take people's homes. I could actually help people; people who for one reason or another were not able to qualify for traditional financing. He left no stone unturned with this program. It was a no-brainer for me. I could be successful beyond my wildest dreams making money while empowering families to achieve the American dream of owning their own home. How gratifying! :-)

Armed with extensive CAHP training, a strong IT background, an unwavering entrepreneurial spirit and a passion for financial literacy, **American Dream Atlanta (ADA)** was born. The company's mission is a lofty one with a client-centric focus. The collective mission of Certified Affordable Housing Provider's is "Transforming Lives through Affordable Housing to Empower Families and Individuals to Enjoy the American Dream of Homeownership". American Dream Atlanta employs a community-based business model which offers clients that are typically underserved by mainstream financing options the opportunity to own their own home. Many of our clients will have the income to support owning a home, but face credit challenges or other issues that would normally disqualify them. This program fills a tremendous void in the marketplace and helps to stabilize communities through pride of ownership.

ADA's Path to Homeownership program offers a stepped approach to homeownership. Clients can begin as renters at the bronze level, or at the rent to own or agreement for deed levels, depending on what they can afford. They can step up to the other levels as their finances permit. This unique program has been adapted to include a client need and affordability assessment, property acquisition, credit repair referrals and financial literacy outreach. Clients qualifying for higher levels of the program are given preferential placement to facilitate the largest number of platinum level achievements.

My purpose now is so much bigger than just "me and money." I aspire to create wealthy minds that create wealthy lives through local partnerships and coaching programs. The approach will be to empower the community to adopt real estate investing as a wealth building strategy.

Doing Good While Doing Well

About Crystal A. Hill

Crystal A. Hill is a longtime Connecticut native who transplanted to the Atlanta area at the end of 2011. She resides with her girlfriend (Janelle) and her daughter (Tania), her niece (Tara) and her two sons (Omie and Richie).

She has 30+ years of Information Technology (IT) experience and started investing in real estate in 2005. She's held Series 6/63 financial licenses, been a Connecticut realtor and member of the Connecticut Real Estate Investors Association. She is a Certified Affordable Housing Provider (CAHP) and also presently holds a membership with both the Georgia and Atlanta Real Estate Investors Associations.

Crystal believes that everyone should attend real estate investors meetings. She feels the education regarding wealth creation and asset protection is priceless and finds it rather unfortunate that fundamental wealth strategies are usually only discussed amongst the affluent.

Crystal is the founder of **American Dream Atlanta**, an organization whose mission is to put families on the path to home ownership, and she is passionate about what she does.

If you're interested in buying property in the Atlanta area, partnering or collaborating with her, you can contact her at **doinggood@americandreamatlanta.com** or call 404.425.9128 x107.

Also be sure to visit her websites at:

www.americandreamatlanta.com
www.metroatlantapropertydeals.com

Chapter 13

It Happened Just Like That!!
By Tina Sharp

"The difference between history's boldest accomplishments, and it's most staggering failures is often, simply, the diligent will to persevere." ~ A. Lincoln

My daughter Breanna was graduating and I needed a gift...a special gift, something with meaning, value, wisdom.

I chose a Christian Book Store; sure they would have some wisdom to depart on my baby as I was preparing to launch her into adulthood. (She was still at that age that she knew everything. You know the age), so I thought a book that she would someday pick up and possibly ponder the words on the pages and take them to heart, and it wasn't coming from her parents.

As I was browsing the book shelves, there were self-help books (God only knows what kind of help she would need once she left home). Naw, the titles didn't quite grab me. Financial books - now that was something I hadn't taught her much about, and her whole future depending on her saving and spending. Ahh, *Rich Dad, Poor Dad*. As I was reading the back of the book of what Robert Kiyosaki had to say about finances, I realized I knew nothing about finances myself, and this would be a great start. He would know what to say to give her direction. Little did I know what this book was really about.

As a concerned parent, I needed to know if this was the kind of wisdom I wanted to depart onto my daughter so I decided to read it first.....Well, needless to say, I had to get her another gift, because I was hooked. She never got the book. I told my husband, Dave, that he HAD to read it. Then I began to get my hands on every book I could by Robert Kiyosaki and passed them on to Dave. Before I could finish one book, he had already bought the next. It happened just like that. He was hooked, too.

Within a matter of months we had to take our other daughter to College in California and being a budget conscious consumer, I had investigated the activities at the convention center in LA to see if there was a convention I could go to in my line of work so I could include it on our trip to get a write off. You guessed it… that led me to one of my first real estate investing seminars. Within months after reading his books, I was going to meet Robert Kiyosaki and learn all about real estate investing….I even came back with a signed autographed "cash flow game" and some new direction and inspiration.

He always said "education would be my greatest asset," so from there my journey began. Just like that. I bought up any program, book or coaching that would give me the education that was driving me to know everything about my new found passion.

I started going to REIA groups to get connected by networking. Now mind you, I am NOT an outgoing person so this was a step that I wasn't fond of, but I pushed past my fear and put myself out there. Did you get that? I put myself out there! With every little "out there" that I put myself, I became more confident.

My daughter Breanna decided not to go to college but to take some time off of school. One day she came home, shocked to see a scene from "a beautiful mind," with pages and pages of the largest poster size sticky notes with formulas, drawings and lists. (My husband and I had just come from a "Rich Dad" seminar and asked for the notes. When we got home we posted them so we could talk about them, ponder them and let them sink in). She thought we were crazy, to say the least, but didn't say a thing, and we didn't indulge in sharing our new passion. She was an "adult" now and we were free to pursue whatever we wanted.

After going to a few REIA groups, a few weeks later with notes still all over the walls, her curiosity finally got the best of her and with concern in her voice, asked what was going on, as we were once again slipping out to go to another REIA group. As we were bustling to get our coats on to scurry out the door, in passing we told her we were going to a real estate investing group and asked if she wanted to go. Of course she wanted to check out what we were so excited about and wanted to make sure we weren't going off our rockers. She said "sure," so she scurried out with us so we wouldn't be late. Then, just like that, one meeting and she, too, was hooked. She caught the passion without any hesitation. (I think it finally all made sense to her)

During one of my REIA events I put myself out there AGAIN and forced myself to raise my hand and be an "idiot" (you know the feeling), in front of a group telling myself "I will learn a lot by this." Well it was true; the questions Than Merrill with Fortune Builders asked me taught me there was still more to learn and he was offering to teach us a new strategy, one I knew was a direction I would want to go because I was already in that type of field. I was going to learn how to rehab and I was going to go to a boot camp! I had never been to a boot camp. Thoughts of tough discipline, no sleep, running laps...I had no idea what was in store for me. I was sooo excited about my future as a real estate investor. So my daughter and I bought in knowing if we did this, we were in and there was no turning back.

Like I said, we were so excited about our new passion in real estate investing that we bought into everything! Boot camp was exciting, got in with a great group of investors who we are so proud to be a part of, who have taught us more than any program or book could about real estate investing. They are on the top of their game. If you check them out, tell them Tina Sharp sent you.

Our first transaction as investors, we bought a little condo and rented out our house and became landlords. Yes, that counts because it gave us education and experience and brings in cash flow and is growing equity at the same time. Our exit strategy: in 2 years owner finance with the Affordable Housing Program or sell the condo to get the next investment.

Our second transaction as investors was when Breanna and I were at a small group for women business owners (once again, pushing past my fear), I had to stand up and tell what business I was in. I stood up and gave my elevator speech, described our cabinet business, what we do and who our clients were and quickly slipped in that I was a real estate investor as well. As I sat down, the president of the group was sitting next to me and patted my leg and whispered that she had a property for me to look at if I was interested and she would even take $50,000.00!!! Oh man, I was so excited, just like that! All I had to do was let someone know I buy houses!! She slipped me the address and I'm telling you, I could not wait to get out the door.

We had learned, "let them name the price first," and she had already named her price when she whispered to me at our first meeting. I gathered all the necessary paperwork that I got from my training and Dave and I nervously approached our meeting. We discussed all we had learned. I asked him what he thought I should offer, and he said, "remember what we learned: if the price doesn't embarrass you, you're offering too much." "Do you think $45,000.00?" I said. "I'd ask $25,000.00" he said. "Really?" I said! "Well that does embarrass me, that's for sure!" "She can always make a counter off and she did say, make an offer," Dave reminded me. OK, we were ready! As we greeted our prospective sellers, papers on the table ready for a deal, I preceded to write down my words of our offer as we spoke. With confidence and eagerness, my prospective seller took my paper and pen and began filling out the paperwork as fast as she could with no hesitation on my offer. She accepted it, no questions asked. WOW! It happened just like that!! Her eagerness frightened me. What did I just get myself into! After talking some more, making sure she didn't want to sleep on it, she confessed she was tired of it. She wanted to move on. She had a lavender farm that she was investing her time and now new money into. I didn't understand because she had a renter in there and was making $600 cash flow. Once again, understanding what we were taught, motivated sellers are the ticket, oh ya...that worked for me. Deal done! We continued to rent to the current renter and collecting the cash flow.

We eventually acquired the house next door, pretty much the same way, only this time using our education to get us private money to purchase and rehab the house. I recognized the neighbor at a community event and mentioned if she was ever interested, I would love to buy her house but I wouldn't pay more than what I paid for the house next door. Turns out, I got it for $20,000.00. It was in bad need of repair, but it was the perfect opportunity to rehab it the way we had been taught.

Doing Good While Doing Well

The economy took a dump and time stole my passion as I vanished into my cabinet business, trying to keep it going. We continued our education sporadically and went to occasional seminars, but fear was setting in and taking over. Breanna got married, had a baby and life was just taking over instead of us taking over life.

I got to a point I couldn't even look at houses for sale or events coming up. Panic set in every time. There was a spark inside that didn't want to die and I knew I would not be happy or have passion again until I was doing what I loved. But now, I just had excuses. Then one day, I heard Lou Brown talking about asset protection in a different way. I had learned about asset protection but just couldn't put my finger on the actual 'how to.' And remember, I had lost my passion. So, I figured I should at least check out how to protect what I do have. I'm telling you, Lou Brown brought it down to my level to fully understand protection and the 'how to,' so once again my spark was getting fanned into a small flame and I was getting my passion back. Then I HAD to put my asset protection in full swing because one of our tenants decided to squat in one of our rentals and he was a smart coo coo, I mean cookie.

Currently, we have sold one of our rentals to an Affordable Housing client by owner financing with Lou Brown's program. Our buyer is so happy she can finally afford a home for her family for the long run.

Our Exit Strategy for our future homes is to use the Affordable Housing Program because it's a win, win. Our buyers win with a home they can be proud of and can afford. We win by knowing we are creating affordable housing for those that want a home, but can't qualify for a loan while building their credit. Another win for us as investors, as it causes our passive income to grow and releases us from landlord responsibilities.

About Tina Sharp

Tina, Dave, and Breanna are dedicated to the development of successful real estate solutions for both families and investors. They have expertise in all aspects of Real Estate and can help you Buy, Sell, or Invest in properties at prices that are tailored to meet your goals. They specialize in purchasing homes and commercial buildings at a fair price and reselling them at below market value to homeowners and investors. Their team will work to make your home and building purchases and sales processes as easy as possible, while providing you with the most up-to-date information of your transaction process as it develops.

Tina's company, **Washington Homes, LLC is a** Real Estate Investment and Management Company for residential and commercial real estate.

They are affiliated with a group of national expert Real Estate investors to better position the company on the leading edge of the real estate market. The company services their clients through Washington Homes, where they conduct real estate investing that benefit home owners and investors in all situations.

Doing Good While Doing Well

Tina and the company offer creative ways for:

- Management strategies
- Alternatives in the ever changing Real Estate market
- Financial strategies
- Business management
- Contracts
- Human resources
- Advertising
- Product knowledge
- Tenant support

To learn more about Tina and her group, visit her at **www.mywahomes.com.**

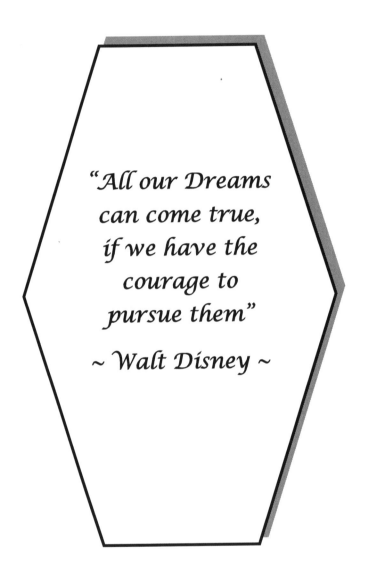

"All our Dreams
can come true,
if we have the
courage to
pursue them"

~ Walt Disney ~

Chapter 14

SUPER SIZE YOUR IRA EARNINGS
By Tony Whalen

"Homeownership is the key to financial stability and wealth building"

Looking back, I guess I've always been involved in the homeownership business. I worked for over 14 years for Schlage Lock Company, the #1 maker of door hardware, in various capacities – lastly being a nationwide corporate trainer.

When I left the corporate world, I moved my 401-K monies to an individual IRA at a local bank. After watching my returns go up and down, eventually diminishing because of stock market fluctuations, I moved my individual IRA to a national firm that specializes in Self Directed ROTH and Traditional IRA's. This "SELF DIRECT" platform provided me with options into alternative investments that generally provide higher rate of returns than I ever saw through the institutional guided IRA management.

This option allowed me the ability to get into Real Estate because it not only gave me the potential to make a good living, but there was the ability to help other people with their housing needs. It all pretty much started a few years ago with a property that I owned.

A few years ago I decided to purchase a single family home that needed extensive renovations, both inside and out. Once the renovations were finished, I was able to market it on the internet, and found a person that needed to live in the exact area, because that was where her job was. She had been looking for some time and we were able to strike a deal on this house where she is renting to own, with the money going towards the principle. She is on a 5 year program, which will then allow her to qualify on her own for a mortgage with a bank.

By doing this, not only was I able to help out an individual that was in need, but I was also able to make a healthy monthly return on my investment. But let me backtrack for just for a moment – I had purchased this house on my own five year program with the owner of the house. Even though I was paying him monthly payments, I was still making a monthly profit. When all is said and done, the owner will make a profit when we close on the house, and I will happily make a profit when my client closes on the house. And compared to what the banks are offering, the percentage on the return on the investment is huge.

I later found another 3 bedroom 3 bath single-family home that I wanted to take on, but needed capital to invest in it. I found an investor who was not happy with the returns he was getting in the stock market, so after some negotiating he decided to come on board and proceeded to invest $40k towards the next property.

Once again this property needed some TLC, but after fixing it up I was then able to move in an individual who also agreed on an option to buy, but this time only 2 years. Not only am I getting a great return on this property, the investor is ecstatic with his return, and has been gracious enough to recommend me to other investors that he knows.

When I initially decided to go full time into Real Estate I did some did training with Lou Brown, eventually becoming a CAHP. One of the things taught in his class was how to take money in an IRA from a traditional bank and turn it into a self-directed IRA, where in fact you are directing that money in different avenues of investment that *you* want to invest in, as opposed to what the banks want. By having a self-directed IRA I have been able to purchase additional homes, tax liens, and have been able to give out personal loans to others to purchase a car, a lawn mower, etc.

I have even been able to help a personal friend set up his own self-directed IRA, and now he is in the process of purchasing tax liens, as well as investing in some real estate properties with me.

Another success story came to me through an ad from Craigslist. A young family was looking to move to the Atlanta area from out of state, but they only had a small amount of money for a down payment, and didn't think they could get a home in the area that they wanted. Through our program I was able to find them a fairly new home in their desired neighborhood and with their new jobs they should be able to qualify for a mortgage on the house within the next three years.

Now here was this young family with 2 small children under the age of 5 who thought their only option was to rent. We were able to set up a deal where they could move in immediately into a home that their family could grow up in, in a great neighborhood and school district that they desired. Not only were we able to provide home ownership, it also provide me and my investor a great investment with a sizeable rate of return.

I continue to find deals, even though I am particular about the type of deals I invest in. But being particular with both my investments and investors has afforded me the ability to successfully grow my company year after year. I look for investors with the right mindset to work with. My ideal investor is an individual that is at least 25 years old, has money in the bank or in the stock market or CD's, is looking towards retirement, and looking for alternative investments and higher returns. This can be money they earned themselves, inherited, trust money, or any other kind of disposable money, with a window of 3-10 years of investing. Depending on what type of return they desire, we are able to pay monthly, quarterly, semi-annually or annually.

These funds invested will be working towards building their retirement. The people that I am really able to help and grow are people working with IRA money, or people trying to build a college fund for a child, for use in maybe 10-15 years. Working with an IRA, funds still grow and compound with no taxes until retirement, or no taxes with a Roth IRA.

Some of the questions I am frequently asked from our investors are:

1. What is securing their money?
2. Do I have current properties they can see that are recently renovated and rented, and
3. How do the properties get managed?

The properties are secured by real property, and I generally have current properties available for show. And most importantly I have a property management company that I am half owner in. So we not only secure the homes and take care of them as far as the investment, we also manage the homes so that we know what is always going on with them. We make sure that they are insured, that everything is covered to provide a safe investment, not only for me, but for the person that is investing. And if the property should pay off early, we have other properties available for the investor.

We are currently rated in the top 5 market places in the USA, based on today's date and growth. Atlanta has a lot of promise in the coming years, as far as new stadiums and new jobs moving into the area. There will be a lot of growth and a lot of people not only moving into starter homes, but moving up into bigger homes as time goes by. So it is the perfect opportunity for investors to get in on base level to get their money working for as long as they want. Even if you live outside of Atlanta or across the great pond, Atlanta is still a great place to invest in.

Doing Good While Doing Well

About Tony Whalen

Tony began his career in Real Estate in 2005 using his IRA money and working part time. He went full time in 2009, leaving a successful 21 year career in the residential and commercial door hardware industry. Tony has done both domestic and international sales along with corporate training experience in this industry.

In the Real Estate industry, Tony has been trained by the most successful and talented instructors, including Lou Brown. He continuously takes classes staying up to date on real estate changes and to stay connected with the many contacts that he has which keeps him in the deal making process. Tony understands the first time home buyer, the move up buyer, as well as the investor. He has been very successful as a buyer, seller, and investor of residential and commercial real estate. Additionally, Tony is well versed in residential and commercial real estate practices. His particular interests are in creative financing deals to include owner financing, foreclosures, short sales, and multi-family housing.

Doing Good While Doing Well

Tony is an investor/partner at GA Housing Property Management, a local property management company in the metro Atlanta area. He actively manages commercial and residential properties of other people as well as his own properties. This keeps him involved in the investor process from beginning to end. He can see any issues before they become problems, keeping the cash flow coming in for the investors and himself. Tony says that it takes positive cash flow to keep the investor and himself paid and happy.

He participates in the local Atlanta REIA, is a member of several investor clubs, and participates in community events. Tony believes in giving back to his community, as his community has given him so much success in real estate.

Over all, Tony has 26 years of Real Estate, sales, business development, and marketing experience to his credit. In short, Mr. Whalen is a successful real estate business person who you should consider talking with to explore the world of better than normal returns on your investments. Tony welcomes any inquiry using the information provided below:

GAHOUSINGPM@Gmail.com

AFFORDABLEHOMES@CHARTER.NET

2451 Cumberland Pkwy., Suite #3753
Atlanta, GA 30339-6157
(678) 793-5012 – Cell

www.BUYAFFORDABLEHOUSING.com (678) 279-3619 –
Buyers Hotline.
www.RENTAFFORDABLEHOUSING.com (678) 279-3619 –
Renters Hotline.
www.SELLAFFORDABLEHOUSING.com (678) 280-2555 –
Sellers Who Want Out Of Their Home.
www.HIGHEARNINGRATES.com (678) 793-5012 or
(877) 209-3943 -   Investors Looking For Better Returns

Tony Whalen - C.A.H.P. *(Certified Affordable Housing Provider)*
GA Housing Consulting, LLC
GA Housing Property Management, LLC

Chapter 15

Why I Chose THE Best Business Model
By Ronald Copelan

"No man can become rich without himself enriching others."
~ Andrew Carnegie ~

At the writing of this book I am almost be 64 years of age. I wanted to make sure that my business model is going to outlast me. In five or 10 years I don't want to start over because I made a mistake and built my business on shaky ground. The Certified Affordable Housing Provider's model for investing in real estate is built on sound economic policies and fundamentally sound principles. I asked myself a lot of questions about what I considered a great model to be. A business trainer/major/ educator would give you a more succinct definition of a great model, but I think you will get a good idea of what I was looking for when you review my list. It is probably more of a list of characteristics than a model or plan. Either way, the *Certified Affordable Housing Provider* and the *Path to Home Ownership* programs are perfect business models.

In my opinion, the following are "must- haves" for a perfect business model:

- Have a business model, plan and system that can weather the ups and downs of the economic cycle.
- Pick a product that will fit the majority of the population. Affordable means "what can your client afford?"
- The product needs to be a must in someone's life, not just a desire. Affordable housing fits that.

- I want the creator of the business model to have been in business at least 20 years and follow his own successful principles.
- I want it to be to be duplicable and scalable. In other words, it should grow in size and profit.
- I want it to be flexible enough to change when the market changes.
- I want it to have an ongoing training program and mastermind group that shares what's working as the market shifts.
- I want it to be capable of being able to hire out most of the business activities while I manage the business.
- I want it to create passive income and to be able to create cash for daily needs.
- I want it to have favorable tax treatment that can be shared with my customers and investors.
- Does it have a solid business plan or their checklists tools manuals for each division of the business?
- Can most of the activities be systematized?
- Does it have forms and contracts that have been time-tested?
- Is it legal?
- Does the industry change so fast that I can't keep up with it?
- Can I be put out of business with the invention of a new product?
- Are the Economic policies fundamentally unsound?
- If I showed it to a politician, would it make them take note and be interested in knowing more? Will my business be of value to him/her?

- If I showed it to my competition, would it make you drool with envy?

On a personal level, it just makes me feel fantastic to know I made a difference in someone's life by providing them with a home. I get quite a rush when people make statements like these to me:

I was door knocking in a particular neighborhood that I like one day. No one came to the door, but I could hear children playing in the backyard. So I went around and knocked on the fence. A young Hispanic guy came out and I told him about our *Path To Home Ownership* program and asked if he was interested in selling his house. "No, I don't own it. I am renting." And then he said, "You mean I could own this home as opposed to renting it? You just changed my grandchildren's' life!" I was perplexed about the reply of "grandchildren." Then I hit me. He was thinking far into the future of his family.

Then there was a Bus driver who said, "I'm 56 years old and no one, not even my family, has ever tried to help me like you have!"

The Benefits of Home Ownership

I will acknowledge that homeownership is not for everyone, and the reasons make sense to me.

But owning your own home... It just makes fundamental common sense if you think about.

Research has shown that our country as a whole benefits from home ownership. In addition, the communities, neighborhoods and individual families reap far reaching social and financial benefits.

And according to the National Association of Realtors' research report in 2012, *Social Benefits of Homeownership and Stable Housing,* we may be changing our nation for the better, one homeownership at a time. The author of the report concluded by saying,

> "Given such an opportunity, public policy makers would be wise to consider the immense social benefits of homeownership for families, local communities and the nation."

Some of the documented socioeconomic benefits include:

1. Increased charitable activity
2. Greater civic participation of local community and national issues (including voting), with enhanced awareness of the political process
3. Maintenance behavior of individual ownership is influenced by those in the neighborhood
4. Higher incidence of membership in voluntary organizations and church attendance with greater attachment to neighborhood and neighbors
5. Greater social capital generated
6. Lower teen pregnancy by children living in owned homes
7. Higher student test scores by children living in owed homes with a higher rate of high school graduation, thereby higher earnings
8. Lower teen delinquency
9. Children are more likely to participate in organized activity and have less television screen time
10. Homeowners take on greater responsibilities, such as home maintenance, and acquire the financial skills to handle mortgage payments, while transferring those skills to the children
11. General increase in a positive outlook on life
12. Homeowners report higher life satisfaction, higher self-esteem, happiness, and a higher perceived control over their lives

Doing Good While Doing Well

13. Better health outcomes, better physical and psychological health

14. Tremendous wealth gain for homeowners under normal housing market conditions (outside of the terrible bubble/burst housing years)

15. Homeowners not only experience a significant increase in housing satisfaction, but also obtain a higher satisfaction, even in the same home in which they resided as renters

16. Family financial situation and housing tenure during childhood and adulthood impacts one's self-rate health (in particular, socioeconomic disadvantage indicated by not being able to save any money or not owning or purchasing a home are less likely to self-rate their health as excellent or very good)

17. Less likely to become a crime victim

18. Homeowners who maintain their homes and high-quality structures also raise their mental health. Renter occupied housing appreciates less than home occupied housing

19. Housing prices are higher in high ownership neighborhoods

With all of these benefits of homeownership, you've got to ask yourself why everyone doesn't buy a house. Most of the time I believe that it is fear or a lack of understanding that keeps a person from even trying. Some of the major issues and/ or questions holding them back include:

- **The Buyer**

    The buyer may feel that he's not going to get a good deal, that he'll be taken advantage of. What if I can't make the payments? What about repairs? They are often confused about what to buy and the mortgage process. I don't have enough money for the down payment. Credit is not good enough to get a loan. What if the economy collapses? Will I be stuck with a house that I do not want?

- **The Seller**

  The seller may think that he will not get top dollar. I'm not going to give my house away. What if I owner finance and my new buyer stops paying? Can I get this house sold before I have to close on my new home? I'm not a salesman, so how I do this? Will the market lose value before I get it sold? I don't have enough equity to sell my house and cover all the selling cost.

- **Private Lender**

  I can assure you that having been a private lender myself, my first and foremost concerned is, will I get my principal back? Will the buyer default? What is my security? Am I at a low enough loan to value that if I have to take the property back and sell it myself will I be able to recoup my principal in any market? Do I know enough about the collateral that I can manage and market it sufficiently to get it sold? Do my borrowers know what they are doing, and will they be able to complete the project in the agreed time frame?

- **Government**

  Is this program real? Do they have sufficient training and experience? Is their business plan and model sustainable? How do I fund it if I want to back the project? Is this a good political move?

Even though the questions and concerns are real, the solutions are easy. Homeownership is an easy process. Just take a deep breath, stay positive, and let me be your problem solver. I can make your problems evaporate so that you, too, can achieve the American Dream of home ownership.

Doing Good While Doing Well

About Ronald Copelan

Ever since 1979, Ron Copelan has been interested in real estate in all of its facets. Everything from options, owner finance, note buying, private lending, commercial, master leasing, wholesaling, asset protection, rehab, management, trust, lease option, and believe it or not, taxes. On an average, Ron's taken at least two courses a year since that date. The principles pretty much stay the same, usually, but the government will impose changes to Laws, regulations and taxes that may have a huge influence on the way you can do business. And you have to keep up with the changes.

At first Ron was interested in medicine and helping people, therefore majoring in biology and pre-med in college. He ended up being a paramedic in Atlanta. Ron and about six other emergency medical technicians became the first paramedics in Georgia. He later moved to Fort Lauderdale, and for 30 more years was a firefighter paramedic for Broward County fire rescue. Ron was one of the medical trainers, a member of the technical rescue team, and retired as a Captain.

Since they worked 24 hours straight and then were off for 48 hours, that gave Ron a lot of time to pursue Real Estate. He managed rentals and bought, sold or brokered private mortgages. He rehabbed and then sold the property. He worked with owner financed houses, wholesales and Lease Options. Ron became a private lender for other Real Estate investors and counsels others on issues of deal structure, negotiation, trust, financing and other real estate related issues.

To learn how you can become a member of Ron's elite group, visit him at:

www.BestHouseDeals.com
www.WeBuyPrivatehouses.com
www.InvestingMoneySafely.com
www.AffordableHousingProviders.org
www.CertifiedAffordableHousingProvider.com

Chapter 16

Equity Based Lending

By Marlen Junck

"The rational thing is to always do what is in one's own long term best interest, and the longest term is eternity."

When banks lend money, they typically rely primarily on the creditworthiness of the borrower to secure their repayment. They will lend 80%, 90%, or even 100% of the value of the property being financed. They lend to people who have a history of paying their bills on time and who can be relied upon to continue to do so - people with high credit scores. When their borrowers don't repay, the banks frequently lose money.

Private lenders, on the other hand, typically base their security not on the creditworthiness of the borrower, but rather on the value of the collateral, or their equity in the collateral. Private lenders will typically lend only 65% of the value of the property being financed, rarely up to 70%. If the borrower fails to repay and the lender is forced to foreclose, the costs of foreclosure and resale do not typically exceed 35% so that the lender can usually recover the entire loan amount, plus whatever interest is owed. The private lender's security is based on his equity position in the property rather than on the borrower's creditworthiness. In addition, because the borrower has a high equity stake in the property, he is less likely to default. Private lenders typically charge a higher rate of interest than do the banks to further offset the greater risk of lending to borrowers with frequently lower credit scores.

What is the benefit to the borrower of these higher interest loans? It is the easy availability of money.

Contractors who renovate residential properties perform a tremendous service to the community. By repairing and upgrading deteriorating properties, they stem and reverse urban, suburban, and even rural decay with all of the benefits that that provides to neighborhoods and cities and other places that people live. Neighborhoods in a good state of maintenance and repair are pleasant places to live for all who are there. Rehabbers increase the supply of quality housing available to all. Rehabbing properties increases the tax base enhancing community tax revenues. Everyone benefits from the rehabber's work.

Rehabbers are often private individuals with limited means. In order to perform their task they need funds to purchase a deteriorating property and funds for building materials, and in many cases for the salaries of employees. For several reasons, banks will frequently not lend to them. The banks' lending criteria have tightened greatly in recent years. Rehab construction loans are something that many, perhaps most, banks simply do not offer. Rehabbers sometimes do not have credit scores considered acceptable by the banks. They frequently do not have the steady income sought by the banks. A rehabber receives his income only when he completes and sells a rehabbed property.

In addition, it can take a relatively long time for a bank to approve a loan. If a deteriorated property is available for a rehabber to purchase, and if he must wait up to 30 or more days for bank approval of his loan, his competitor may well have bought the property before he has the funds to do so. This is not good for the rehabber's business.

Private lenders lend to rehabbers, and they lend quickly.

A rehabber who uses his own funds must complete and sell one project in order to raise the funds to begin the next. If he has employees, his crew may be idle while he sells his renovated home and searches for and acquires another deteriorated property on which to work. He may have to pay his crew during this time in order to keep them available, even though they have no work to do.

With a loan from a private lender, the rehabber can acquire his next property before he completes his current one. He can keep his crew fully occupied at all times.

Private equity loans can also be utilized at times by real estate wholesalers, those who locate deteriorated properties and pass them on to rehab contractors.

The private equity rehab loan is frequently for a term of six months, occasionally up to a year. That is all the time that is usually needed to renovate and sell a private home. These loans mature too quickly to be affected by changing real estate markets. Even in severe downturns such as that a few years ago, real estate prices do not change fast enough to jeopardize a six month loan significantly.

The private lender's position is secured by a mortgage on the property, just as in the case of a bank. The title company pays off the mortgage from the proceeds of the sale when the property is sold.

If the borrower needs a loan for more than 65% of the value of the property he is purchasing, he may offer other properties which he owns as additional collateral. These would also then be included in the mortgage. The mortgage is prepared either by a title company or by an attorney who does title work.

There are a great many laws and regulations which apply to loans on owner occupied residences which do not often apply to properties undergoing rehab. The rehabbing contractor does not typically occupy the property. His activities fall under laws pertaining to commercial enterprises rather than owner occupied housing. One result of this is that the time to foreclose if the rehabber fails to pay his loan on time is often shorter than it is for an occupant of a home who defaults on his mortgage.

There are commercial mortgage brokers who introduce rehabbers needing money to lenders with available money, and who complete much of the paperwork and other arrangements necessary to the lending process. These are not the same brokers who find mortgages for owner occupant buyers. Commercial mortgage brokers do not find loans for owner occupant borrowers, and owner occupant mortgage brokers do not deal in commercial loans.

The commercial mortgage broker will frequently obtain the borrower's credit report, although this is not a major factor in approving an equity based loan. If the same borrower returns for a future additional loan, the credit report will be on file and will usually not again be sought. The broker will obtain a loan application and will order an appraisal of the property. He will also obtain a preliminary title report. He will make these available to interested private lenders until one of them commits to funding the loan. He will then cooperate with a title company in arranging a closing.

The borrower will pay for expenses associated with the closing, such as the appraisal and the title services. The broker will usually add several points (a point is 1% of the loan value) to the loan to cover his fee.

Sometimes borrowers and private lenders will become acquainted through such events as local real estate association meetings. They may then use an attorney instead of a commercial mortgage broker to complete their paperwork.

If you are a borrower seeking a private equity loan, you may find a private lender or a commercial mortgage broker at a real estate association meeting. If you are a lender, you may find a borrower or a broker who has borrowers available at the real estate meeting. In addition, Real Estate associations in your area can be found by internet search.

Now there are businesses which have been founded for the purpose of private equity lending. One of these is our company, **Private Finance Solutions LLC**. Not only do these companies provide necessary loans to rehabbers and other real estate investors, but they can also be a source of investment revenue for individuals with savings who might like a better return than they are now achieving, yet without sacrificing a great deal of safety.

The stock market has dropped by as much as 50% at times, and individual stocks often drop even farther. Losses of that magnitude in short term mortgages on real estate at a conservative loan to value ratio are rare.

Most fixed income investments are paying very low rates of return at this time. Money market rates and bank CD rates are less than 2%. Private equity lending can provide much higher returns with relatively low risk.

If an individual with funds in an IRA or 401K or other savings vehicle is to participate with a private equity firm, there are formalities to be observed. There are state and federal regulations designed to protect the investor. These must be complied with. If you are interested, more information can be obtained at our web site **privatefinancesolutions.org**.

We wish you the best of success in all of your investment and real estate endeavors.

Doing Good While Doing Well

About Marlen Junck

Marlen Junck is a long time real estate investor and founding member of Wisconsin Real Estate Investment Group LLC and Wisconsin Real Estate Investment Solutions LLC. He manages Private Finance Solutions LLC, a private equity lending firm.

His first real estate investment was a small 8 unit apartment complex in the early 1980's. He has bought, sold, rehabbed, and rented residential real estate intermittently since that time.

He developed a stock investment strategy which netted average annual returns of over 13% for over 25 years, limited to investing in undervalued high grade blue chip stocks. This has allowed him to personally make over a million dollars in the stock market.

Marlen has also been in the active practice of medicine for 45 years. He has practiced radiology for over 40 years in Wisconsin and Michigan. He derives a great deal of gratification from the ability to help other people in need.

He was a Viet Nam combat veteran with the Riverine forces in the Mekong Delta and received the Navy Commendation Medal with

Doing Good While Doing Well

Combat "V" for his services in Viet Nam. He was the primary medevac officer on the Cambodian border and triaged and provided initial medical care to battle casualties, calling in medevac helicopters. He visited local Vietnamese villages, providing medical care to the residents. The Navy cited him for saving the lives of several Vietnamese children.

For many years, he has operated a dairy farm in southern Wisconsin, following the tradition of his grandparents. He now lives on a small lake and enjoys boating and water sports.

He is an avid nature lover and wildlife photographer. He has an extensive collection of wildlife photography.

Marlen has 5 children, all with doctorate degrees in law, dentistry, psychology, or medicine, as well as 12 grandchildren.

To learn more about how Marlen can help you, visit him at his website at **privatefinancesolutions.org**.

Chapter 17

Choosing To Succeed

By Elizabeth A. Brown

"When you are looking for something more in life, try helping someone else uplift their life. Just remember there is a difference between help and interference."

CHOICES... Some people look back on their life and think "How did I get here?" Others examine their current situation and wonder "Where do I go from here?" Then there are those who assess their progress towards achieving their goals and ask "What are my next steps?"

I have experienced each of those crossroads numerous times. I find myself asking those same questions or several variations of the same. Regardless of the type or the frequency, it all boils down to the fact that we all make choices throughout our lives which have resulted in us being exactly where we are, doing exactly what we do. Sometimes we feel our choices are beyond our control. But when we honestly drill down to the truth of the matter, our own self-directed choices have brought us to wherever we are. As with many, my choices have been influenced by how and where I was raised and grew up.

I was raised to believe that if you work hard and apply yourself, you could achieve anything. For the most part, that was true. What wasn't discussed, but understood, was that there will always be some that will be privileged, having advantages, placement and standing that will give them more, whether they work for it or not. Therefore, not having to work for it left some of this privileged few, ignorant of the need for many to have to work hard and struggle to obtain a fraction of what many of the privileged elite take for granted. Those who were not raised to understand 'with great privilege came great responsibility' could become callous, insensitive or downright disdainful of those who did not have as much as they did.

I prefaced my story with the aforementioned observations to give you insight to how I came to be where I am, and doing what I am doing as a Certified Affordable Home Provider. I worked hard and received scholarships, grants and loans to obtain undergrad and graduate degrees. I achieved these degrees while working full time at night. I moved up through the ranks in Corporate America, using the social, psychological and political tools I learned along the way. I liked helping others get out of their own way, so that they could obtain their upwardly mobile objectives. While I didn't help others expecting to get something back, I found that I really enjoyed seeing others achieve their objectives. My only request was that they help someone else along. Most complied with my "help someone else" platform. The result was that I was able to move rapidly up the career ladder by turning around the morale, efficiency and operational performance of troubled facilities.

That was the case when I accepted a job in Milwaukee, Wisconsin. They had experienced a devastating workplace violence incident, and they were at the bottom of almost every measureable category. Two years later we were in the top 10 of every measureable category. Another two years and a promotion later we were in the top 3 of every measureable category. Having an interest in real estate, once things became stable, I began to look into investing. I did well with residential investing. I then ran into a "perfect storm" of real estate investing devastation. I took on

146

my first high dollar commercial property investment. I later found out that the property had not been inspected or open for operation for over 8 years, so there was no certificate of occupancy. I trusted the Lender's property evaluation. I did not protect myself from the work the Seller had done without a permit, prior to the closing. Then the overstated real estate property values crashed. Also, I had taken out a second mortgage on my primary residence. Once again choices were made… unfortunately they were bad choices. Learning the hard way is very humbling and expensive.

Almost seemingly simultaneously, my career ascent then hit an invisible ceiling and my work environment became frigid when I refused to take another "lateral" move, even if each offer did include more money and a larger platform. Since it did not seem that I would be achieving my next career objective any time soon and I needed a way to get my "helping others" fix, I did a self-assessment. My hard work resulted in having several options. I had a golden parachute executive retirement package. I could opt out of the Executive Track while retaining my salary, benefits and retirement package and take any position, anywhere, with full executive relocation benefits.

But thanks to real estate's "perfect storm" crash, this was looking less like a viable option. The devaluation of my primary resident, now with the second mortgage, definitely put the kibosh on relocation as a viable option. So I took another position where I was currently working.

Refinancing became a popular option for those with underwater mortgages, so I attempted to refinance, per the Homeowners Act. First, I was informed that I could not apply for refinancing under the Homeowners Act unless I was delinquent, although they would never provide that response in writing. I investigated the Homeowners Act and discovered that free counseling was available to assist homeowners. When I went for an intake session, I noticed they were overwhelmed with the number of people seeking assistance. I had time and interest in doing something more. Plus, I needed to get my "help someone else" fix. So I volunteered to become a Foreclosure Avoidance provider. I took the 4 days training and paid out of pocket for travel and lodging, (something I never had to do in the last 20 years), passed the test and got started as a Certified Foreclosure Avoidance Counselor. I couldn't wait to begin "helping someone else." Unfortunately, reality came quick and harsh.

Despite the intent, the Act had no teeth. The Banks and Mortgage Services had the process, paperwork, websites and the scripts to assist Homeowners in distress to avoid foreclosure. However, it was all for show. I saw people lose their homes for a difference of as little as $15 in their monthly payments. Your big Banks and Mortgage Servicers had numerous call centers established across the country. But every time you called to follow up on a case, even after you submitted documentation that you were a certified counselor with an accredited non-profit organization, you got the 'phone tag' run-around. Since you were never provided a contact person or number, once a file was established we counselors wound up spending our time faxing and re-faxing documents to various processing sites. I never experienced a mortgage reduction in the year I worked with the group.

In fact, the majority of the cases were in what I called the "Spin Cycle." Spin meaning the Spin the public was given so that Homeowners could actually be given an opportunity to save their homes from foreclosure. The Spin that mortgages were actually being modified by forgiving the underwater portion of the current property value, in a forbearance. The Spin that mortgage rates and/or payments were being lowered to assist the Homeowner in avoiding foreclosure.

I thought I worked with a systemic bureaucracy in my corporate job. Those banks showed me. So I "chose" to stop "Spinning" my wheels and proceeded to find a way to actually help people save their homes or move on to something more affordable. So after attending numerous real estate seminars, with various gurus espousing numerous variations of systems and schemes that seemingly only work for those who are getting those checks they include in their presentations, I then attended a Lou Brown webinar.

You need to understand that although I had previously been successful in residential investing, I had become totally disenfranchised and disillusioned when I tuned in to hear Lou Brown. At the time, I rarely listened to real estate webinars anymore. And I definitely hadn't made it through to the end of one, in over a year. In fact, the only reason I even signed up to attend was because a successful real estate investor I knew highly recommended him to me.

The Counseling experience had left me in a "why bother" state. After all, how can you help people when the system put in place by the government to help them is being totally disregarded? Well, imagine my surprise when I heard this man talk about how he got started and achieved what he had achieved in various real estate markets... all without banks. HELLO. He was now preaching to the choir.

Doing Good While Doing Well

Even though I had a healthy dose of cynicism, the more I listened to Lou, the more I started to review his materials. He explained every step you needed to take, clearly and concisely. He provided the game plan, the checklist for whatever game plan you chose to use, and presentation guidelines. Lou's courses are actually training courses... with him teaching... ALL THREE DAYS. He only invites speakers to speak that are in alignment with the session he is teaching, and are in compliance with the Street Smart level of expertise and customer service.

I was proceeding cautiously, adding more course as I liked what I saw and that was being delivered. And then Lou started talking about Quiet Title. He had partnered with a Non-Profit company that not only knew about the Banks' "Spin Cycle" but they had the entire history, laws and documentation about the entire Commerce, Investment and Banking Industry. In fact, the Quite Title Session educated me into understanding that the "Spin Cycle" was just a tiny, infinitesimal tip of the iceberg of manipulation, deception and corruption. DING! DING! DING!

I was now all in. I can invest in real estate without banks. I can actually help people again. And I have expanded the scope of who I can help. Previously, I was certified to assist just those who were about to lose their homes to foreclosure. Now, as an Affordable Housing Provider, I am in a position to help so many more. I am excited at all of the possibilities. We have home buying programs with multiple options helping distressed homeowners find the solution that works for them. We have the Path to Home Ownership program, which provides viable options for those looking to buy their first home, downsize or even upsize their home. We not only provide the physical house, we also incorporate credit building in our home ownership program, a stumbling block to many hoping to become a home owner. We are not just trying to sell a property. We are building relationships to meet the housing needs of our customers, their family and friends for a lifetime. We also help private investors get a consistently greater return on their investment than they would achieve in a bank account, CD or stocks.

It is not easy letting go of the familiar and going full steam ahead with an entirely new way of doing things. At least it was new to me. Just last year I had two cash buys fall through because the Bank with the REOs wanted to know all the individual members of the LLC and the individuals involved in the trust. This was after providing documentation that the LLC had the funds in the account and those funds had been there for a while, and providing the LLC's Operating Agreement Article authorizing a corporate bank account and the purchase of real estate. Did I mention that this was a CASH purchase? The icing on the cake was when the Real Estate Agent that was supposed to be representing me asked why we had a problem providing the names of the members of the LLC. What was I trying to hide?

Every step of the way, my attempts to hang on to remnants of doing things the old way have run smack dab into seemingly insurmountable obstacles. My Mother used to say that "...a hard head makes a soft behind." Meaning you keep falling on it, exposing it by continuing to do stupid things or things which do not work. So picking myself up and dusting my "behind" off, I am now ALL IN as a Platinum Certified Affordable Housing Provider.

As an ALL IN Platinum Mastermind member, I now bounce my deals and questions past Lou and the Platinum group. I must say that out of all of the acquaintances I have made going to the various real estate seminars and associations, our group has some of the most knowledgeable, successful, savvy and helpful members I have had the pleasure of meeting and working with. I look forward to being a part of our nationwide movement to take the Street Smart Affordable Housing Provider and Path to Home Ownership Programs to the next level...as nationally recognized brands.

Doing Good While Doing Well

About Elizabeth A. Brown

Elizabeth was born and raised in Chicago, IL. After graduating, she joined a corporate management track program. Navigating her career throughout the Midwest, she has lived and purchased residences in Louisville, KY, Washington, DC, St. Louis, Mo, Kansas City, KS, Wichita, Ks, Topeka, Ks, and Atlanta, GA. There was even one stint back in her hometown of Chicago. While intrigued with the ever increasing appreciation of her housing dollars with each promotion and relocation, it wasn't until she slowed down in Milwaukee, WI that she decided to act upon that interest. That interest resulted in the purchase of a few single family and small multifamily rentals. However, she soon came face-to-face with the harsh reality if investing due to the residential property market crash beginning in 2006. Having placed a 2nd mortgage on her primary residence, she found herself personally experiencing an upside down mortgage. When investigating the Homeowners Assistance Refinancing Program, she realized that while she understood the process, and was blessed to have the resources to navigate through the chaos successfully, many did not. That led Elizabeth to get involved with helping people try to avoid foreclosure, which eventually led to becoming a Street Smart Certified Affordable Home Provider.

Elizabeth is a Managing Member of Allcrest Affordable Housing, LLC. Her passion and commitment to helping others obtain their dream of homeownership have resulted in others joining her effort. The demand and opportunities are great and unending.

You can connect with Elizabeth (Liz) directly at **allcrestllc@gmail.com** for more information on how you, too, can join the ranks as a Certified Affordable Housing Provider, or visit **www.yourhouseloansolution.com.**

Chapter 18

The Journey Starts With an Idea

By David Grace and Jim Lamarr

"Change one person and you change the world"

Project Outreach, Inc. is a non-profit organization co-founded by Jim Lamarr and myself with the mission of providing safe, clean, secure, and affordable special needs housing for veterans, the homeless, those in recovery, and other "returning citizens." Jim and I came together from very different backgrounds to unite and form Project Outreach. Based in the Boston area, Project Outreach now holds and operates six properties which provide affordable housing for more than 70 residents. Our short term goal is to expand to 200 residents locally, while our long term goals are to provide other types of specialty housing and to show and teach others throughout the country what we do, thereby expanding our mission in a more powerful way.

In our group housing, for all new participants, we offer first step sober housing. We provide in-house meetings and assist residents by guiding them toward financial literacy training, further education, medical resources, and counseling. The houses provide fellowship and more importantly *HOPE,* as they rebuild their lives and reintegrate into society. As residents progress we have the ability to offer graduate houses, rental units and home ownership programs.

Job opportunities are a key to the success of our residents. We assist with resume preparation and job placement. We are also able to hire a number of our own residents to assist with the management and maintenance of our houses. We also hire residents and provide on-the-job training in the construction trades as we rehabilitate our own properties that we acquire for our affordable housing programs.

As part of our diversified funding plan we accept monetary gifts and donations from individuals and organizations, as well as gifts of clothing, food, furniture, computers, and anything else our residents may use in rebuilding their lives. In addition, we can accept charitable gifts of Real Estate. Project Outreach collaborates with a nationally recognized expert who assists in educating individuals, community leaders, and organizations with their questions related to the charitable gifting of Real Estate while facilitating the donation of these gifts. Real Estate donations do not necessarily need to be suited for use as resident homes directly, they can be anywhere in the world and may include commercial property, residential property, or land. These Real Estate assets can be converted to assets that benefit Project Outreach beneficiaries directly.

Doing Good While Doing Well

David's Story

As far back as I can remember I had always been interested in how things were put together, in working with my hands, and in building things. These traits are probably what led me toward a career in dentistry. While in school, in addition to my studies in the sciences and dentistry, I also received degrees in business management and economics. I think a hidden entrepreneurial spirit attracted me to those subjects. So, like most entrepreneurs, I figured out at an early age that I didn't want to work for anyone else but myself.

After my training and internships were over I went in to private practice. I opened my own office in the Boston area where I grew up and have spent nearly three decades doing dentistry there. Over the years as I treated my patients, I noticed many of the people who were born and raised in the area were not able to afford to stay in the area.

This included young people trying to start out on their own, seniors who came to rely on fixed incomes, and those who had experienced some sort of personal or family hardship.

These observations, coupled with a chance happening led me to become involved in housing and real estate in my community. I was attending a 3-day Dental conference and on the last day the final speaker of the meeting was scheduled to talk on the subject of real estate. This presentation, which was the only one of the entire 3-day meeting on a non-dental related topic, made me curious, so I decided to stay and listen. He spoke on the use of non-traditional techniques of real estate investing. I found the topic and information presented extremely interesting, and I was hooked. Over the next 1-2 years I did research, attended real estate seminars, webinars, read and listened to everything I could to learn all I could about buying, selling, holding and investing in real estate. This in turn led me to meeting Lou Brown, getting involved in his real estate training and becoming a Certified Affordable Housing Provider (CAHP).

This training and what I have learned has allowed me to help sellers get rid of problem properties, help buyers get into homes that they otherwise couldn't qualify for, and help other investors not only earn better and safer returns on their investments, but also give them the satisfaction of knowing their investments were being used in helping others.

One great example of how all this can work took place during one of those cold New England winters a few years ago. I had purchased a house as an estate sale. It was in terrible condition and the heirs, the son and daughter of the deceased owner, were actually embarrassed to show the house to anyone because of the poor conditions their father had been living under. They had been estranged from their father for several years but still did not want others to see the condition of the property. I was the first and the only potential buyer to see the property. I purchased it quickly, solved their problem, had the renovations done, and put the property up for sale using the "Path to Home Ownership" techniques taught in the CAHP Program. A few days later I was contacted by a gentleman who lived in the same neighborhood. It turned out that his mother had passed away recently and he was having their home remodeled, which had been in the family for many years and they had shared together before her passing. One of the workers had accidentally set the house on fire. It was a total loss, and had to be torn down immediately. For three weeks in the middle of winter this man had been living with his two dogs in a trailer he owned, parked on the property, because he had nowhere else to go. His insurance proceeds were not going to be enough to rebuild, and he wouldn't qualify for a new loan due to some past credit issues. But because his income and the size of his down payment qualified him with our Affordable Housing Program, he was able to move into this home just two days before Christmas, using our rent-to-own program. Eighteen months later his credit had been repaired and now qualified for financing, he exercised his option to buy the home.

Another property I came across had been vacant for 14 years; this property was a mess both inside and out. The owner had been paying the mortgage and had kept all the utilities on all that time without even living there! The property was the subject of litigation with the city and the case dragged on for all those years. The homeowner had just lost her final appeal and now wanted to get rid of the property and all the stress it had caused her. For this property I called on multiple techniques from my CAHP training. I purchased the property with no money down, subject to the existing $130,000 mortgage. In other words, I took over the payments on the existing loan and the seller agreed to wait for the balance of the purchase price until I renovated and sold the property. For the $75,000 it would take for the renovations and the carrying costs I was able to use financing from a private lender. Once renovated, the home was placed on the market and I was approached by a couple with two young daughters at an open house we held. They were very interested in the home but could not qualify; not because they had poor credit, but because they had *no credit*. They had lived in this country only a few years and never had financed anything before, had no credit cards, no bank accounts, and paid for everything with cash. I found that they could qualify for our Affordable Housing Program called "Path to Home Ownership" as they had enough income and down payment to afford this home. In fact, they were able to give a very large down payment for this home, the largest down payment I had ever received for a single family home: $100,000 toward a purchase price of $328,000. They purchased the home on an Agreement For Deed, which meant we would finance the remaining $228,000 due on the home for up to 2 years, until they could get a conventional loan. Twenty-two months later they got their financing, the original seller and her first mortgage loan had been paid off, and the private lender was paid back the funds he loaned along with a portion of the profit for his return.

These new residents, along with several others residing in the properties I have been involved with, have expressed to me how they feel they have received something valuable, and have been extremely thankful. I am the one that should be most thankful, for I feel I have received far more value than I have given.

Doing Good While Doing Well

Jim's Story

As David previously mentioned, my background is quite different from his. To be honest, my background is quite different than most. I grew up in Boston during the 70's and had a typical Boston family. Well, typical around here means dysfunctional, to say the least.

My father worked on the trucking docks and my mom was mostly a stay at home mom and from an early age I was confronted with alcoholism and addiction, diseases that had destroyed my family. I first noticed this in 1976 when my grandfather (Papa) had died and although I was too young to understand, I would quickly find out about the cunning and baffling disease of alcoholism. My grandfather died of cirrhosis of the liver and I lost my fun and go lucky Papa to this horrible disease. This same disease was waiting in the wings to do more and more damage to my family and me. I grew up as a normal kid and loved sports and was very active as a young boy with sports and school but family issues and the thousand forms of fear alcoholism and addiction disguised itself in quickly took a hold of me. My parents divorced when I was a young teenager and I starting to fade away from sports and school and quickly found myself dropping out of school in the ninth grade. The streets became both my playground and my teacher and I had many years of struggles growing up. The school of hard knocks is where I got my education, and I am so grateful for that now, although I wouldn't suggest it to most people as it was a very difficult journey, to say the least. By the grace of God I got sober in the mid 90's when I was in my early twenties and the seed of recovery was planted and my new journey began. My daughter Kelsey was born in 1993 and my life changed forever.

Doing Good While Doing Well

For the first time in my life I had this burning desire to change and be a good dad and a good person; it was my mission. It took some trial and error and I struggled for a few more years but in 1998 I met my beautiful wife Shannon and my life's mission changed again.

I taught myself everything I know about business. I had always worked in the construction business and I also had a burning entrepreneurial spirit. I wanted to be successful. So I formed my construction company and was ready to take on the world.

I would quickly find that all life's lessons and hard knocks I suffered growing up were the perfect training ground for business. I received my MBA on the streets of Boston. I worked harder than everybody else I knew because I had to; this was my only way to overcome the hurdles I had created for myself and get ahead. My business thrived, we had one heck of a reputation, we conquered every job put in front of us from small additions, to remodels, to building houses and we were quite good. My wife and I went on to have three beautiful daughters, Samantha, Casey and Jaime and all seemed great on the outside, but something was missing.

I found that to keep it you must give it away. I know that sounds a bit strange, but I needed to give back and that's what started the next chapter of my life. An idea came to me to start Project Outlook, a "how-to guide and manual" to operate specialty housing. So I set out to open my first house. I called it the 12 Step House. I leased a property in Boston and outfitted it with beds and furniture and set out on my journey to help other men in recovery. The house quickly filled up and I was on my way. I learned from my mistakes (is there any other way?) and I adapted the program at every step. I then went on to form the Lower Mills Community Realty Trust and opened up five more buildings in Boston and adapted my program and called it Project Outlook. It was growing and adapting to help people in need. I was also getting great rewards personally from helping others (that's the secret).

I knew a lot of people in Boston and was entrenched in the recovery community and this little idea I had quickly started to bloom, but it was missing a crucial piece: the perfect partner. As fate would have it I met Dr. David Grace at a local REIA meeting here in Boston and we hit it off right away. I ended up doing some remodeling work for him on some of his investment properties. Dave and I got talking and I told him about what I was doing and our passions to help people collided and I quickly found that we had a lot in common. Dave and I got to work and quickly formed our non-profit called Project Outreach and incorporated my manual. I had already been working with veterans in recovery so it was seamless to modify our program and mission statement to help our veterans with housing needs. In the near future we would like to expand our specialty housing model by offering housing for autistic residents, handicapped accessible housing and are rising up to meet the other challenges we see in the specialty housing community.

We currently have six houses in and around Boston, and as we write this story we have approximately 75 beds available and we are now completely full. Considering we just started together a year and a half ago, we are truly blessed to have this success. As is paramount in any business, it has taken complete dedication, building a great foundation, and incorporating a great program. We are now looking for additional properties and the referrals are coming in in droves. We hope to expand from 75 beds to 200 beds in the next 12-18 months and to start to develop our own buildings to meet the needs and challenges of our clients. I can't wait until the next challenge as the road ahead always changes, but if you're willing to rise to the challenges and help others along the way, anything is possible.....Jim L.

Doing Good While Doing Well

About Jim Lamarr

Mr. Lamarr is involved in several outreach programs that help Veterans in Recovery find help and resources, education services, fellowship, and housing. This outreach has been expanded to incorporate specialty housing, disability housing, sober housing and associated services. Mr. Lamarr recently Founded 12 Step House, LLC in December 2011 and is currently operating a sober recovery home for men.

Mr. Lamarr has also been working for several years developing a program called Project Outlook. This program is basically an operating manual and bylaws to operate specialty housing projects. This manual can be incorporated to run and manage various types of specialty housing.

Mr. Lamarr co-formed the Lower Mills Community Realty Trust in January 2012 which has taken over five properties in the Lower Mills area of Dorchester, Massachusetts. This property is currently being used to house Veterans in recovery and men in recovery, but also can offer standard Veterans housing. This program has also attracted many inner city neighborhood services and Veterans affairs groups to help enhance the quality of life for our Veterans.

Mr. Lamarr is the founder and current President of J.M.L. Custom Building & Design Inc. which was incorporated in 2007 in Massachusetts as an S-Corp. JML is a full service general contracting company specializing in all forms of new construction and remodeling & rehabilitation work. Mr. Lamarr, his wife Shannon and their three daughters live in Canton, Massachusetts.

Mr. Lamarr is the founder and President of Lamarr Folkman development group LLC with Paul Folkman which was incorporated in 2013 in Massachusetts. Lamarr/Folkman is full service real estate Development Company specializing in all phases of development. Lamarr/Folkman specializes in identifying property and permitting to establish highest and best use for a particular property. Lamarr/Folkman has several large condominium projects under way including a 28-unit condo development with David Grace as our partner/investor, as well as a 30-unit high end town house development in Boston. We are also permitting a nine house sub-division and several six to sixteen unit apartment and condominium projects.

Mr. Lamarr is also the co-founder of "We Salute You Veterans" a non-profit organization formed in 2012 to help homeless veterans with emergency needs such as clothing, boots, meals, hats and gloves, as well as fund raising and offering other needed services and housing. Jim founded "We Salute You Veterans" with Scruffy Wallace of the famed Boston band, the *Dropkick Murphys*.

Doing Good While Doing Well

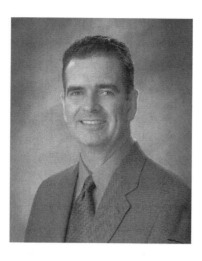

About Dr. David Grace

Dr. Grace has spent over three decades helping others in his community. He got his start as a healthcare provider practicing dentistry with the US Public Health Service and with the Veteran's Administration. He later went into private practice in the community where he was raised and now resides.

Among Dr. Grace's many professional affiliations are active memberships in the American Dental Association, Massachusetts Dental Society, American Academy of Implant Dentistry, and American Academy of Cosmetic Dentistry. He also has been awarded Fellowship status in the Academy of General Dentistry. Dr. Grace has published several white papers on a wide range of dental topics.

Over the years as he treated his patients, Dr. Grace observed a need in his community. He noticed many individuals who were born and raised in the area were not able to afford to stay in the area. This included young people trying to start out on their own, seniors who came to rely on fixed incomes, and those who had experienced some personal or family hardship. Those observations led Dr. Grace to seek training and to become involved in housing and real estate in his community. He has earned the professional designation of Certified Affordable Housing Provider (CAHP) and is a member of the Eastern Massachusetts Real Estate Investors Association.

This in turn led to Dr. Grace's co-founding of Project Outreach, Inc. a non-profit corporation with the mission of supporting safe, clean, and secure special needs housing for veterans, the homeless, those in recovery, and other "returning citizens." Today Dr. Grace uses his 30 years of business, healthcare, and housing experience to further the mission of Project Outreach in his community.

To learn more about Project Outreach, visit **www.ProjectOutreachBoston.org**

Chapter 19

Creating Those Win-Win Opportunities

By Matt Vile

"You were born to win, but to be a winner, you must plan to win, prepare to win, and expect to win." ~ Zig Ziglar

I like to win, but I also like other people to win. I'm the type of person who likes everybody to come out on top. I don't like lose-lose or even win-lose. I want to win and I want everyone who deals with me to win as well. I even named my companies *Win Win Real Estate, LLC,* and *Win Win Investments, LLC* because I like the idea of creating those win-win opportunities.

By day I'm a computer programmer, and I enjoy it, but the problem is that it is a job and therefore requires active participation. If I don't go to work I don't get a paycheck. It's active income. At one time this used to be a win-win situation for me because my schedule was very flexible. My company cared more about deadlines and production and less about me being in the office. They didn't mind if I worked from home or worked odd hours, as long as I made my deadlines. But due to acquisitions over the years, I now work for a large corporation which requires my presence during business hours. Don't get me wrong...I enjoy what I do, but without the flexibility that I once had, coupled with the fact that it requires active participation to generate the active income, this has lost its win-win status.

But real estate....here's an opportunity for not only me, but for perspective homeowners and sellers to come out winning. I started studying real estate in 2005 and back then I suffered from "paralysis of analysis." Making sure I had all my ducks in a row. Spending my time analyzing the processes and the systems, ensuring I had contingencies for every possible situation, putting my "dream team" together. I would gather contacts for realtors, accountants, bankers, lawyers, plumbers, electricians and the different trades that I might need. I developed a business plan and created my LLC. I spent a year studying and analyzing. Whew! But it all paid off.

I bought my first house in Norman, a college suburb just south of Oklahoma City, in 2006. Back then, being more flexible, I could be more hands on and actively participate in the home repairs myself.

It's always been my intention to buy and hold rentals to take advantage of the passive income and the wealth creation that holding real estate brings. The monthly cash flow, the equity build up, and the debt pay down are some of the passive benefits of holding real estate. Helping people solve problems, whether they are selling, buying or renting is rewarding, too. Each house is a nice story in and of itself. Some of them have been homeruns. Some of them have been challenging and didn't go according to the plan. Fortunately I did my homework and patiently waited for the deals that provided the wiggle room needed to account for the unplanned obstacles. Although some houses have gone better than others, even the worst scenarios have worked out, because buying real estate right is my key to this business.

But good deals don't just fall in my lap. I look at a lot of houses and I make offers on all of them. If I take the time to look at a house, I've made it a rule to at least make an offer that is accepted, even if I don't really want the house. My wife is picky when it comes to houses and she has said many times "do not buy this house," and I will respond with "not even for a hundred dollars?" and of course she would say "yea, for a hundred" and then I'd say "what about two hundred?" and we would go back and forth. The point is that there is an amount I can offer that makes sense for me.

I tend to buy most of my properties through wholesalers. They tend to understand the numbers and what they need to be for it to be a win for me (and them). I've built a reputation locally for being a solid buyer that can close on the offer that I make. I love to buy property 'subject to' the existing mortgage. When I started investing in real estate 'subject to' was my preferred way to buy homes and I even bought some of them from wholesalers, some of them from marketing and others from word of mouth.

I get plenty of calls...from people wanting too much, thinking that a couple of thousand dollars' worth of equity in a $150,000 house was a sweet deal, or dealing with realtors that think $10,000 off of a $150,000 house is a home run deal. When I throw an offer out there I do get some hang ups or doors slammed, but I'm not scared of hearing no. It's just one more on my way to my next 'yes.'

Wholesale deals are good. I let those guys do the work, and I'm not scared to let them make some money. I've certainly given out big wholesaling fees, because I'll make an offer. I don't care what their numbers is. I once paid $15,000 as a wholesale assignment fee, because it was right for me.

'Subject to' is a bit of a hurdle when you're talking to a seller. I generally will lay out a couple of offers, a cash offer, or what I call a seller finance offer. My intent with regard to the seller finance offer is to get it 'subject to,' but I broach the subject with a "would you be willing to entertain a seller finance offer? Because I can generally give more, depending on the underlying mortgage," or better, yet there is no mortgage.

I had a wholesaler call me once said he had a house for me. It was a four bedroom, two bath house in Norman, Oklahoma worth about $120,000. He wanted $55,000, so I was very interested and went over to take a look at it. It was a complete disaster. Everything in the house was broken, roach infested and dirty. As the seller (who was living in the house) showed me around I talked with her about the possibility of taking over the payments and giving a little more. She didn't care, she just wanted cash. So I met with my wholesaler and we signed a contract to close within 30 days. I was getting a hard money loan to close this deal, so I needed to put that together, so that was going to take a couple of weeks to process.

So as I'm putting the hard money together, the wholesaler calls and says the seller really wants to close by the 1st, which was five days away. I didn't think I could hurry the hard money lender that fast so I brought up the subject to offer again. If she would be willing to sell it to me 'subject to,' and sign the note over, then I could close it within a few days. And she agreed, as long as we could close before the 1st. She didn't want to make another payment on the house. Like I said, it was bug infested, with windows and doors broken. It was in total disarray. But we closed it by the first. I took over her note and went in and fixed it all up. This house has been a home run from the beginning and I was able to help this lady out of a bad situation.

Doing Good While Doing Well

I like it when things come together. I also like it when I win and I'm not even the highest bidder! Recently I closed on a house, and I was actually the third bidder. The first buyer actually backed out by not showing up to Title Company for the closing. So there is the wholesaler and the seller at the title company waiting on the buyer who doesn't show. How embarrassing. The wholesaler was frantically making calls to try and salvage he deal, as the wholesaler's time was running out. He called me and of course my cash offer was good and I told him I could close anytime. He still called a higher bidder but that buyer couldn't close quickly. And so we closed 2 days later. He was so thankful to me for being able to close and so apologetic to the seller that day. He even made several thousand dollars.

That very scenario has played out more than once, where I'm the 3rd bidder in a "highest and best" situation, and in the end, they call me because the other two can't close. I actually love it when that happens. They are super motivated by then and next time they call me first.

Sellers sometimes have to have a dose of reality and be softened up by the market. One house came on the market through the MLS and I went right over to their open house and chatted with the listing agent and told them I would give them $175,000, which was 70% of the value. I remember the comment she made that the owner wasn't stupid or crazy and I got the impression that she thought I was one or both. I didn't know it at the time but she told me later that the listing agreement required her to have an open house every two weeks until it was sold. And so, I would go by and say 'hi' and let her know that my offer was still good. After 6 months they were ready to accept. This was an expensive house for me and so I had an inspection done. They were so motivated they covered everything the inspector found. That house is a home run.

Now I will admit that my offers probably aren't the best ones, but they are solid. Since I bought my first property in '06 I've established solid connections with some of the local banks. And my model these days is to either to buy them 'subject to' or for cash. If I buy them for cash then I fix them up, put a renter/tenant buyer in them, and then refinance them ending up with more cash than I began with. Now that's a multiple win situation. Wax on, wax off, rinse and repeat,

As I wrap this up I would leave you with a few parting thoughts: Integrity is a must. Truth is the best defense. What good is it for a man to gain the world but lose his soul? My word is my bond. Pigs get fat and hogs get slaughtered (don't be greedy). Be a servant. Be a problem solver. Make the uncomfortable calls first. Take action every day. Surround yourself with people who are doing what you want to do or at a place you want to be. Invest in yourself. Believe!

Doing Good While Doing Well

About Matt Vile

Matt has a Bachelor's degree in Business administration in Management information systems with a minor in economics from the University of Oklahoma. He currently works a full time job as a Programmer Analysis specialist. He became a real estate investor in 2005 and buys increasingly more houses every year in order to produce passive income and build wealth while providing quality housing at affordable prices. He is very active in several of the local real estate investor associations. He believes emphatically in education, training, systems and networking. He is a certified affordable housing provider through the Street Smart Affordable Housing Network.

Matt and Katrina Vile live in Norman, OK. They have six children and 5 grandchildren.

Matt@WinWinRei.com

www.WinWinRei.com

www.SellOKCMetroHomes.com

www.BuyOKCMetrohouses.com

Chapter 20

Because I Said "Yes"

By Janice Brown

Do or Do Not.. There is No Try ~ Yoda

I married into real estate. My parents were homeowners but not investors. I wasn't interested in real estate and had no concept about what it entailed, how to do it, or even why anyone would be interested. When I left college my plan was to change the world through social work.

That didn't turn out so well.

First there were, at that time, no jobs available in social work. I guess I was not the only person who left college, figuring they could fix the world. Second, government didn't seem to have the money for new positions or new ideas. Third, I discovered the world didn't really want to be fixed – even with my great ideas. So, I got a job in retail management because the company needed women managers. I discovered new worlds for my social work experience. I discovered that social work is actually a good foundation for managing people.

It was while working in retail that I met and married Lou. This is also when I met real estate for the first time as an intimate part of my life. Where Lou is, so there dwells real estate. He went to seminars and read books. I didn't. He bought courses and studied. I didn't.

He bought more courses and went to more seminars. I didn't. He faithfully attended the monthly real estate association meetings. I didn't. Lou began his career as a full time real estate investor just after our daughter and second child Diana was born. I went to work at a job as a medical social worker. He volunteered and then became a Board member at the local real estate investors association. I did go to the picnics with Lou and the kids. He became a member of RELAA. I couldn't remember what that stood for. He transformed it into National REIA. I thought that was a good idea because then I could remember what it meant and the discounts he planned for the memberships sounded really good for us. The whole point is real estate was Lou's thing. I really didn't consider it as that big a part of my little world until Lou and I talked about Lou going into real estate investing full time. That caught my attention.

We talked about it. A lot. We had sold one business and his staying self-employed didn't upset me. We talked about the money that would be involved and the time and the energy. I supported it because I knew Lou loved real estate investing and he would be good at it. I had no idea where that simple agreement would take me.

My job as a medical social worker gave us some income and most especially it provided health insurance for us and our kids. Real estate impinged on my life in odd ways. We would cruise his neighborhoods on our way home from church and sometimes looked at houses. Some weekends we would spend cleaning a house to get it ready for a new tenant. The kids even worked, too, and earned some spending money. At some houses toys would be left and for those we got an amazing amount of work out of a 4 and 5 year old. He spent a ton of time volunteering and building GaREIA (Georgia Real Estate Investors Association) and then National REIA. Occasionally, I would type letters or contracts. I still remember typing my first legal description. I am dyslexic and that paragraph of feet and directions and turns and degrees was a nightmare.

Then our kids got old enough to start school. And I wanted to be home for that.

So Lou and I had another talk about how our life could look should I decided to leave my good job and stay home. Lou offered me this fabulous part time, temporary job. I would do the paperwork, and answer the phone and look through the ads in the paper and just assist Lou. This sounded good to me and I took the job.

Then Lou gave me my first contract to do.

As far as I was concerned, it was a blank sheet of paper. Three blank sheets of paper. I had no relationship with it. I had second thoughts about this fabulous part time job.

However, we persevered and got through that and learned how to work together and started an amazing journey together that has resulted in a business that not only pays the bills, but allows us to help others and contribute to our community.

I evolved into being in full time charge of our property management. There are things about my job that can drive me totally crazy. They're called tenants.....wait, no, clients. My clients can make me unbalanced at times. The phone ringing off the hook can become irritating. The water department, code enforcement, trashed houses, court, trying to get employers and previous landlords to call me back, getting contractors into tenanted houses to do repairs...I could name a few more dozen things that can get me going.

Doing Good While Doing Well

You know what makes it worth everything? It's not just the money coming in.

It's the feeling I get when I KNOW I've put the right family in the right house. It's the feeling that I made a difference in someone's life who never dreamed they could own their own house. It's driving down a street in a neighborhood where we've renovated several houses and seeing how the neighborhood has changed. That's happened to me many times now. It's just a great feeling.

It's Leon that makes it all worthwhile. He's 63 and never owned his own home. He's been in his home now for 9 months. He's still amazed it's happening. His son called me because he wants the same deal. We're looking for a house for him now. So far nothing has fit, but the right house is coming. Leon moved in his house and did our 'Work For Equity' program. The down payment credit he earned is more than he will need and Leon is getting together his paperwork to apply for a bank loan. He loves to show what he did to his house, not just the work for equity work, but what he and his wife did to make that house their very own. They'd never been able to choose their own paint colors before.

It's Tara Bell that makes it all worthwhile. She's a single nurse who wanted her own home but didn't know how she could afford it. She did the work for equity program as well and sent us pictures of her dream kitchen when she got it done. Her kitchen island is a work of art. She exercised her option, stepped up, and is now a Gold level member. I've urged her to take that last step, but she's more comfortable staying with us, she says.

It's people like Willie and his wife that make it all worthwhile. They walked into the office and asked me if I had a house for rent. Willie said he wanted to be upfront with me and told me they had been dispossessed in the past. They looked beaten down and hopeless. I told them that if I had a house that rented for 1/3 of their monthly income and they would agree to payroll deduction, I could rent them a home. I don't think they really believed me but put in their applications anyway. I sent them to two houses and they fell in love with one. Willie painted the house inside and out and also put in a privacy fence. By the time they had moved in and lived there for two months, they didn't look like the same people. That's the difference a home can make.

It's Miss Mary that makes it worthwhile. Miss Mary came in to apply for a house for herself and her 15 year old son. She wanted a better place to raise him than an apartment. She was concerned she didn't have enough money to buy, but after we went over the path to ownership, she was convinced she could. And excited about it. Her son wanted nothing else for Christmas but their house. Their whole Christmas was moving into THEIR house.

It's people like Carolyn and her husband that make it all worthwhile. She came into the office to talk to me and went to see nearly every house I had available in inventory. It took weeks for her to make a decision. What I didn't know was she was having a difficult time getting her husband to believe we would work with them on getting them into their own home. He kept telling her since he was self- employed they'd never get a loan. He

kept reminding her we could be a scam. He told her they didn't have enough money saved and they would have to wait a while. When she told him about the work for equity program, he finally called me. After we finished talking, he and Carolyn decided on a 4 bedroom home where he did the painting inside and out and installed the new a/c unit as he is an HVAC guy. The house is the one Carolyn went to see every week. They are very happy with their new home and I am very popular in their family.

It's people like Deirdre who make it worthwhile. Deirdre came to the office after a friend of hers told her about our program. Deirdre had just inherited 4 children and desperately needed to move from her 2 bedroom apartment into a house that would accommodate her new children, plus her other one, and her. We went through the inventory since she needed to move immediately. I had the perfect house already in inventory and move-in ready. Deirdre wanted a large kitchen so the kids could do homework while she worked in the kitchen and her house has that and a lot more that she wanted. Plus she needed a house the social worker would approve of and her house is a home the social worker approved. The kids like living with their aunt. That's the difference the right home can make.

As for family, it's hearing my 17 year old son say thank you because he had just seen the Great Pyramid. It's sitting on a wall in Machu Picchu and remembering my twin and I planning a trip to Peru just for Machu Picchu. It's watching my nine year old daughter's face when the guide at Tulum told her Mayan dancers got paid in chocolate but got killed if they made mistakes. It's walking around Ayers Rock with my dad after his telling me for decades he was on his way to Australia. It's talking with Lou's aunt in Edinburgh, Scotland about her speaking with Princess Diana the day the Princess visited the school she cooked at and watching Lou and his newfound cousin discuss nefarious plots they could have done had they known each other as boys. It's seeing my foster daughter on the Grand Staircase on a cruise ship and realizing her mother would love that picture and making sure her mother got it. All of those moments and more that enrich our family's lives are what makes it worthwhile to be in real estate investing.

What makes every day worthwhile is our conviction that not only are we helping people by providing them the opportunity of home ownership, but knowing we stabilize neighborhoods as owners (and those planning to be) are more invested in their homes and neighborhoods than renters. What makes every day worthwhile is the funds we can donate to the charities we feel make a huge difference in our communities. I feel it is a privilege to work in a business that allows us to enjoy life as well as helping people and communities while we do so. It is FUN to help people realize their dreams.

And to think all this came about because I had the intelligence to say yes when Lou asked me to marry him. I don't even want to think about what life might be like if we had never created a family and a business like this together. We are truly blessed!

Doing Good While Doing Well

About Janice Brown

Janice was born in Kentucky and raised in Texas, Florida and Kentucky. Her father graduated with his doctorate when she was ten. Her mother dropped out of college when she was a freshman and she was a sophomore because German was beyond her and she called the health class teacher an idiot because she got twins out of the rhythm method and wasn't going to let one child lie to babies about the facts of life. Janice is an identical twin and yes, she had fun with that when they were kids.

Janice graduated with a BA in sociology and psychology with a minor in juvenile law enforcement. She is also within 4 hours of completing her Master's degree in social psychology. She has worked as a juvenile high risk youth center manager, a manager in retail merchandising, a medical social worker, and a property manager. She never bought a house and is not an investor. Janice manages, sells, rents, leases, and leases to own property.

Janice got into property management through marriage. She married Lou Brown in a moment of sheer brilliance without knowing what she was getting into by marrying him. She has traveled to Europe, Asia, Africa, South America, Central America,

Australia, and New Zealand and driven through a lot of the USA. She has seen the Grand Canyon, the Great Wall, Machu Picchu, Uluulu (Ayers Rock), the Pyramids, Jerusalem, waded in the Atlantic in Florida and in the Atlantic in Nigeria, danced with a blue footed booby in the Galapagos Islands, and visited the Great Barrier Reef. She has seen cathedrals and castles all over Europe and stood in the Parthenon in Athens. She's walked in Trafalgar Square, Tiananmen Square, and Times Square. She's walked along the Seine, the Yangtze, the Mississippi, the Nile, and the Hudson rivers. She's boated down the Rhine River and would love to boat down the Amazon.

Janice has watched two children grow into amazing adults and a foster daughter find her place in the world. During all that she watched an amazing man teach himself the art of investing and the science of building a business and then proceed to develop systems to train and share an amazing business opportunity with thousands of other people.

Janice is thankful she had the sense to marry him.

"*The secret of success is to be ready when your opportunity comes.*"

~ Benjamin Disraeli ~

Made in the USA
San Bernardino, CA
22 March 2014